TEARS OF ZION

Divided We Stand

Ya'acov (Yana) Liberman

University Press of America,® Inc.
Lanham · Boulder · New York · Toronto · Oxford

Copyright © 2006 by
University Press of America,® Inc.
4501 Forbes Boulevard
Suite 200
Lanham, Maryland 20706
UPA Acquisitions Department (301) 459-3366

PO Box 317
Oxford
OX2 9RU, UK

All rights reserved
Printed in the United States of America
British Library Cataloging in Publication Information Available

Library of Congress Control Number: 2006922462
ISBN-13: 978-0-7618-3457-1 (paperback : alk. paper)

⊖™ The paper used in this publication meets the minimum
requirements of American National Standard for Information
Sciences—Permanence of Paper for Printed Library Materials,
ANSI Z39.48—1984

This book is dedicated to

the fallen disciples of Jabotinsky's Monism,

Martyrs of Zion

and

Victims of Cain

Contents

Part 1   **The Cain and Abel of Zionism**

1	By Way of Introduction	3
2	The Arlozoroff Case	11
3	The Evacuation Fiasco	19
4	American Jewry During the Holocaust	27
5	Divided They Stood	35
6	Season of Treason	45
7	The Tragic Road to Victory	53
8	"Altalena"	61
9	Twenty Years of Tears and Errors	71

Part 2   **Political Upheaval in Zionism**

10	Blood and Tears—Victories and "Earthquake"	81
11	Siding with the Enemy in Peace and in War	89
12	Competing for Peace	99
13	Zionism on Brink of Disaster	109
14	The Dangers of Today	115
15	Beware of Tomorrow	123

Index   129

About the Author   135

Part 1

The Cain and Abel of Zionism

Chapter 1
By Way of Introduction

Zionism's political left, now scattered by the winds of self destruction, can be found not only in the Labor Party of Shimon Peres, but also in the outdated Peace Now Movement, Yossi Sarid's Meiraz Party and Yossi Beilin's group of Don Quixotish peace makers.

Strangely enough, it was born from within the bubble of pure Marxism, embracing Theodor Herzel's aspirations for Jewish statehood on one hand and Lenin's theory of collectivism and proletarian dictatorship, on the other.

The Movement had its achievements and produced historic figures such as Dr. Chaim Arlozoroff, David Ben Gurion, Moshe Sharet and others. From inception it dominated organized Zionism, often with a positive and productive influence on the development and realization of the Jewish national dream. On the other hand it had never compromised its social and leftist philosophies which prevented a genuine unity and integrity of the Herzelian political movement.

Rapidly, their influence grew and their representation multiplied within the ranks of the Zionist Organization. Gradually, due to divisions and personality clashes, the socialists split into several groupings eventually to be recognized as Mapai, Mapam and Ahdut Avoda.

Born on the stage of European anti-Semitism, as illustrated by the historic Dreyfus trial and Tsarist pogroms, Herzelian Zionism was much more than the reflection of Dr. Herzel's belated recognition of Jewish homelessness being the cause of relentless persecutions and deprivations of Jewry, worldwide.

Without the support of Russian and East European Zionists, Herzel would have remained a lonely voice, ignored if not opposed by the "reforming" Jews of Western Europe.

Together with the participation of politically intelligent Jewish leaders from Russia and Poland, Herzel found the necessary numerical following that was sorely lacking among the Jewry of France, Germany and Austria. However, these leaders from the East were anything but monolithic in their interpretation of Zionism's goals, methods and character.

In the early stages of Zionist political activity, Herzel attempted to bring Turkey into accepting the notion of Jewish autonomy in Palestine. Having failed in this effort, he began to look elsewhere for an alternative. It was at this point that Britain offered Uganda and the first serious clash occurred between the majority of Zionists who saw the fulfillment of their national dream only in the land of Zion, and the minority, whose prime interest lay in salvaging Jewry from lands of pogroms and discrimination. The majority, heavily supported by Russian and Polish Zionists, won that debate and began to realize the ultimate dream by providing pioneers, ready to colonize and industrialize areas in Palestine that were settled by them, usually with the aid provided by Jewish philanthropists such as Baron Edmund James de Rothschild of England.

With the death of Dr. Herzel in 1904, the Zionist Movement he created could boast of concrete achievements in Palestine, especially in the area of pioneering and creating settlements with Jewish youngsters from Russia.

After Herzel's death the leadership of the Zionist Organization moved from Austria to Berlin. From Berlin, Austrian and German Jews were at the helm of the movement while its numerical strength continued to come from Russia.

It is important to realize that at this time the Russian Jewish masses were subjected to a strong influence of the revolutionary ideals of socialism. Thus many became convinced that the Jewish People could exist as a distinct national group in the Diaspora, in countries of Jewish dispersion. These Jewish socialists flocked to the Bund, founded in Russia in 1897. Ten years later, another group of Russian socialists were organized as Zionists under the name of Poale Zion (Workers of Zion).

These Russian Jews were equally impressed with socialism and Zionism. It was their conviction that leftist ideology could be constructively applied to the ideals of Jewish statehood in Palestine. Their first world conference was held in The Hague in 1907.

By this time however, with the failure of Russian Revolution of 1905 and besieged at home by ever more ferocious pogroms, the Jewish youth of Russia became progressively disillusioned with the prophets of Jewish emancipation within Eastern Europe. They began, in ever growing numbers, to immigrate to Palestine and to live there as pioneers, in newly founded agricultural settlements, within the environment in which they planned to merge their nationalist and socialist ideals.

Thus, by the outbreak of World War I, there were more than 90,000 Jews living in Palestine. There were some forty Jewish agricultural settlements with a total of 13,000 settlers. Most of these settlements were generously financed by Baron Rothschild.

However, in spite of being a minority even among Jews, these settlers and their leaders came to control Jewish organized life in Palestine.

In the meantime, with Turkey siding with Germany, an opportunity offered itself for "political Zionism" to re-assert itself by aligning with the British. As a result, the center of the Zionist movement shifted from Germany to Britain. From here on, the leadership was relayed to Jews of Russian origin living in London. The foremost among them were Prof. Chaim Weizmann and Nahum Sokolov, both of the Algemain Zionists or the "General Zionist Party".

The General Zionists and the Socialists of the left found it advantageous to cooperate in sharing the leadership of the Zionist Organization. Its economic and financial strength came from Jews of the United States and Britain, whereas the rank and file was mainly composed of Jewish socialists from Russia and Poland.

In spite of their influence and growing control of political, economic and social life in Palestine, the socialists of Poale Zion were not the only organized Jewish force in the Ishuv of Palestine.

Thousands of orthodox Jews, especially in the area of Jerusalem, were deeply involved in promoting the welfare and education of orthodoxy. Their political leadership was concentrated in the hands of the Mizrachi Organization. Since they were basically interested in promoting adherence to Talmudic teachings, it was possible and advantageous for them to cooperate with the dominating force of the socialist leadership.

The fourth element in the growing Zionist Movement belonged to the nationalists, who soon became better known as the Revisionists, under the inspiring leadership of Zeev (Vladimir) Jabotinsky, a young Zionist from Odessa. Since the Revisionists stood in direct opposition to the leftist philosophy of the socialist Zionists, the rivalry between them was sharp and often bitter. On the other hand, the Algemain Zionists of Europe and Russia provided the aura of internationalism on matters concerning Jewish statehood. Remaining clear of fundamental ideologies of either right or the left, they were more comfortable being allied with the socialists rather than supporting the more militant and assertive Zionism of the Revisionists.

Nevertheless, until the culmination of the first global conflict in 1918, the four major forces of the Zionist Movement, the Algemain Zionists, The Socialists, the Nationalists and the Orthodox lived and worked side by side, jointly promoting the overall interests of the political Zionist Movement.

Now, with the advent of the British Mandate in Palestine, the ideological lines began to become more pronounced.

Interestingly enough the major clash between the Left and the Right did not occur on the subject of socialism as opposed to capitalism. These were merely side issues left for cultural meetings and inter-party debates. The first and major political confrontation involved the very essence of the Zionist Movement: The final aim of political Zionism!

The First World War was also instrumental in Jabotinsky's creation of the Jewish Legion within the framework of the British armed forces. In this venture, he was closely assisted by his personal friend, the one armed Jewish hero of the Russo-Japanese war, Yosef Trumpeldor and the British Colonel Henry John Patterson.

When the war ended, many of the demobilized legionnaires remained in Palestine and together with non-socialist pioneers, students and entrepreneurs, became the core of Jabotinsky's Revisionist followers. They and those that eventually joined them were relegated into a permanent minority among the Ishuv in both Palestine and the Jewish State, for more than fifty years.

However, in the earlier days following the British adoption of the Balfour

Declaration, the divisions among Jews in Palestine were obvious but less threatening. In fact, it was at this time that Jabotinsky and his legionnaires were able to form, unopposed, the first Jewish resistance force which they called the "Hagana" (Defense). It was from this force and bearing the same name that the later Hagana of the Jewish Agency was created and which eventually became the predecessor of the Israeli Defense Forces.

Initially, it was Jabotinsky himself who led these self-defense forces in Jerusalem during the Arab pogrom of Passover in 1920. For this effort, the British penalized him with a fifteen year sentence of hard labor. Subsequently they released him, prohibiting his re-entry to Palestine, for life.

However, in 1921 Jabotinsky was still very much a part of the World Zionist Organization. In fact he was soon elected to its executive. This did not prevent him from voicing a strong resistance to Britain's increasingly anti-Zionist attitude as well as his demand for a stronger Zionist reaction.

By 1923, Jabotinsky realized that he was being restrained in his activism and decided to resign from the executive. In the meantime he organized a nationalistically minded youth movement called Brith Trumpeldor, after his heroic friend Yosef Trumpeldor. (The movement was also called "Betar", named after Bar Kochba's last stronghold).

Now, the lines between social and national forces in Zionism became clearly drawn. The differences emerged with Jabotinsky's complaints against inaction and appeasement. He and his followers were strong believers in decisive action against Arab pogroms. They advocated outspoken opposition to British curtailment of Jewish immigration to Palestine and demanded a clear statement to the affect that the primary aim of Zionism is the establishment of an independent Jewish State in biblical Eretz Israel.

At the outset, the Left, often known as the Labor Zionists, restricted their opposition by sharply criticizing his policy and his methods. Jabotinsky, on his part, continued traveling and promoting his views on how to translate the Zionist dream into reality. He openly advocated that the key to statehood is a Jewish majority in Palestine and solicited in favor of illegal immigration.

The Labor Zionists were driven to actual anger and resentment, as Jabotinsky stressed the need to encourage large scale immigration of the middle class to Palestine. And although Jabotinsky and his followers accepted the idea of a welfare state, they remained strongly opposed to the creation of a totally egalitarian society with no reward for individual initiative.

This was now much more than a political debate. Here, in this confrontation of ideological principles, the dominating Labor Zionists in Palestine felt threatened by an open influx of middle class Zionists, not necessarily adherents to their social and political philosophies.

In the meantime the danger of Nazism grew and embraced all of Western Europe. While the Labor-led Zionist Organization continued its routine activity, the Revisionists saw the imminent peril. Accordingly, the Revisionists embarked on an open confrontation with both the British and the leaders of the Zionist movement. Jabotinsky personally led the campaign, exhorting Jewish youth to make this illegal immigration a national Jewish sport! Soon Jabotinsky's only son, Errie, was assigned to organize boatloads of Jewish pioneers to cross the Mediterranean and land "illegally" on the shores of Palestine.

As public support of Jabotinsky grew, opposition to him and his Revisionist Party became both bitter and ugly. Not only Jabotinsky himself but also his elderly mother were targets of abuse and denunciation by the leaders of social Zionism. Consistently he was labeled as fascist and accused of spreading unwarranted panic among European Jewry. Even his efforts at illegal immigration were condemned as a stab in the back for organized Zionism.

(Only a few years later, the "official" Zionist Organization took upon itself, the task of illegal immigration, which it continued well into the post World War II period. Of course many thousands of Jewish lives could have been saved if this belated effort would have begun earlier . . .)

Gradually the popularity of Zeev Jabotinsky grew in direct proportion with the spread of Nazism and the ever-growing realization that not only Jews from Austria and Germany but also those from all over Europe, were in mortal danger.

In fact, as early as 1931, the Revisionists gave a real scare to their socialist adversaries by gaining 21% of the Zionist Congress vote against 29% obtained by the Labor.

It was at this time that the political disagreement began to turn into an ugly contest for power, snow-balling into the first case of a blood libel wherein the Left accused the Revisionists of murdering Dr. Chaim Arlozoroff, head of the political department of the Jewish Agency.

Although the accused *betarim* Abrasha Stavsky and Zvi Rosenblatt were acquitted by a British court after two Arab thieves admitted to murder, the poisonous seeds of the libel created a climate of unprecedented hatred against all followers of Zeev Jabotinsky, for generations to come.

With time, this hatred grew into a self-destructive political cancer causing pain and frustration to the great Zionist cause. It eventually backfired and destroyed the hegemony of Social Zionism. On this long road of divisiveness and fraternal enmity, serious errors of judgment also contributed in inflicting grave pain to the cause of Zion.

It should be noted that back in the thirties; the leaders in both camps realized the potential disaster of this development and tried to soft pedal the dangerous confrontation. In fact, both Ben Gurion and Jabotinsky attempted to reconcile the opposing elements by negotiating a Labor agreement between the Left and the Right. However, the majority within the Labor party was totally opposed to any such reconciliation.

Within two years, in 1935 in Vienna, at a Revisionist Congress representing seven hundred thousand members, the Revisionist Party severed all relations with the Zionist Organization and announced to the world the emergence of the New Zionist Organization.

The following four years were consumed by a mass tragedy of European Jews and the dark advent of Nazism in Europe.

By now, there was hardly a Jew left who did not realize that Jabotinsky's prophesies were correct and that Europe was on the abyss of destruction while its Jewry was on the verge of a total catastrophe. But even this did not neutralize the hate which consumed the Left wing of Zionism. Even at this, eleventh hour, they could not breach their total rejection of the Revisionists in order to form a united defense against the murderers of their People.

Indeed, even in the underground in various death camps, especially in the Warsaw Ghetto, Jews fought in separate units, under separate commands, until the very end.

This painful internal strife within Zionism was vividly mirrored in the vast Jewish community of American Jewry. Here too the passions of envy, jealousy and hate played havoc with the spirit of Jewish brotherhood. Following the lead of the socialist leadership of the Zionist Organization, American Jewry tilted heavily in favor of accommodation, appeasement and socialism of the Labor Movement. Their vigorous struggle against the Jabotinsky Revisionists was just as bitter and no less cruel.

But it all began on June 16, 1933 when the Arlozoroff blood libel succeeded in portraying Labor Zionists as "moderates" and the Revisionists as irresponsible hot heads. And this lasted for 44 years!

In June 1948 – 15 years to the month after Arlozoroff's tragedy, another murder took place. Only now, both victim and the perpetrator were clearly defined. This was the case of "Altalena", when Prime Minister Ben Gurion ordered his lieutenant, Itzhak Rabin, to fire at the "Altalena" which was approaching the shores of Tel-Aviv with volunteers and armaments destined for Israel's defense. "Altalena", a ship bearing the name of Jabotinsky's pseudonym and commandeered by the Hebrew underground, the Irgun (National Military Organization inspired by Jabotinsky in addition to the Revisionists and Betar), was brutally attacked by the newly formed army in contravention to an existing agreement.

When Ben Gurion was taken to task for this fratricide by members of the coalition of his newborn government, he sardonically replied: "Blessed be the gun that shot the *'Altalena'*" (By tragic coincidence of fate, one of the "Altalena" victims that fell from Ben Gurion's "blessed gun" was none other than Abrasha Stavsky of the Arlozoroff days . . .)

When Menachem Begin, commander of the Hebrew Underground, the Irgun Zvai Leumi, addressed the citizens of Israel explaining the circumstances of this murderous assault, he was derided by the supporters of the Prime Minister for sounding tearful and weak.

The truth is that Menachem Begin, who went through the worst Siberian prisons and successfully led a victorious Hebrew Underground against the British Empire, did shed tears in revealing the depth of the fraternal assault, during which, once again, Cain rose against Abel and, once again, "thy brother's blood cried unto me from the ground"![1]

These tears were the tears of a nation mourning its loss of innocence, the sacredness of fraternity and the depth of its faith. These, like many other tears caused by greed, ambition and rage are the most painful of tears, for they are shed in sorrow rather than anger, in pain rather than hate. These are pure tears, the tears of Zion.

Such tears of Zion have accompanied Herzel's political Zionism from one generation to another for more than half a century.

Notes

1. *Genesis* 4:1

Chapter 2
The Arlozoroff Case

June in Tel Aviv can be a very warm month. But the evenings are usually pleasantly cool, especially by the sea shore. A good time to stroll on the beach.

It was that kind of evening, June 16, 1933, when Dr. Chaim Arlozoroff, "one of the brightest and best of the rising stars of Mapai", [1] was walking on the beach of Tel Aviv, discussing with his wife on the heavy and deep impressions he collected during his recent fact-finding mission to Germany. He was delegated there in his capacity as head of the political department of the Jewish Agency (the executive arm of the World Zionist Organization).

As evening shadows covered the moist layers of the golden sands of the beach, the couple was suddenly accosted by two men, one of whom drew a revolver and shot Arlozoroff point blank in the chest.

The screams of Arlozoroff's wife drew the attention of some distant by-passers, and eventually of the police. The perpetrators disappeared quickly, while the victim was taken to a nearby hospital, where he was pronounced dead.

Although murders of Jews in Palestine were a frequent occurrence, these were always connected with the usual tension between Jew and Arab. However, with no basis in logic, the entire Labor Zionist Movement directed its collective suspicion upon the Revisionists. In this, they found immediate sympathy and understanding on the part of the British administration, which did not seem to be interested in examining other possibilities or in looking elsewhere for the culprits.

By morning of June 19th, the police were knocking at the apartment of the editor of the Revisionist weekly, "Hazit Ha'am" (the People's Front), Dr. Abba Achimeir. There, they bumped into a young *betari*, Abraham Stavsky, who arrived from Poland only three months ago. Within moments, Stavsky was placed under arrest.

By July 22nd, twenty more Revisionists were arrested. One of them was Zvi Rosenblatt. All were confronted with Mrs. Arlozoroff who identified Stavsky as "resembling the companion of the man who fired the shot" and Rosenblatt, as "the man who fired the shot" [2].

Immediately following the arrests of the two, the Mapai leadership through its control of the Jewish press and radio, began a bitter and far reaching campaign accusing the two *betarim* of murder and censuring the entire Revisionist Movement for provocation and complicity.

Both Stavsky and Rosenblatt vehemently denied having been anywhere near the Tel Aviv beach at the time of murder.

The Revisionist Movement, led by Jabotinsky himself, accused the Mapai leadership of perpetuating a blood libel and sought to provide the accused with the best possible defense.

In the meantime, two Arabs, Abdul Majid and Issa el Abrass, confessed to the murder. In court they admitted having attempted theft, but panicking when Mrs. Arlozoroff began to attract attention with her screams.

The British Court refused to believe the confession and even went as far as to induce the confessors to withdraw it.

The police adamantly stuck to their blind accusations of Stavsky and Rosenblatt. This, beyond doubt, was a direct result of the enormous public campaign waged in Palestine and abroad, which centered on the aim of persuading the public that the crime is a Revisionist one. Even the official report of the Mandatory Power, made to the League of Nations for 1934, found it appropriate to say: "Rightly or wrongly, the crime (Arlozoroff's assassination) is ascribed to Revisionist preaching against what that Party is said to regard as the timorous methods of the Jewish Agency"[3].

In the meantime, the atmosphere of violent animosity permeated Jewish life in every corner of the world. But nowhere was the hate as deep and the antagonism so dangerous as in Palestine and Poland.

Socialists were joined by Itzhak Grinbaum's General Zionist group named Al Hamishmar (on guard). Together, they issued a statement calling for the wholesale outlawing of the entire Jabotinsky movement: "We declare that the moral responsibility for this brutal assassination falls upon the entire Revisionist movement, which has produced such a murderer.... Whoever is still concerned about the fate of Zionism, must shake himself clear of the Revisionist past. No intercourse, whatever with Revisionism! Let our motto be: 'Expel the Revisionist gangs from Jewish life' "[4]. And all this before the verdict was even reached.

To this Jabotinsky reacted with a powerful statement to the international press: "I feel sure that both Stavsky and Rosenblatt are innocent and it is evident that the investigation has so far produced no proof that has a chance of convincing any unbiased court of their guilt. We will stand by these innocent men as my generation stood by Mendel Belies (a Kiev Jew who, in 1913, was accused by the Czarist authorities of committing a ritual murder on a Christian youth Andrei Yushinsky, but was acquitted by the jury)."[5]

In the meantime, the provocations and the campaign of hate were re-focused onto the person of Jabotinsky himself. Daily, he was accosted by socialist gangs, insulted in public and, on various occasions, attacked physically. In Kaunas, a hail of stones greeted his car, accompanied by shouts of "assassin" and other such epithets, according to recollections of his late biographer.

Mordechai Katz.

This was the environment and the atmosphere on the eve of the 18th Zionist Congress. However, in spite of all the negative press and public campaign against the Revisionists, they received 96,818 votes as compared to 55,848 in the previous Congress. Certainly, the atmosphere and the mood in the halls of deliberations at the Congress were conducive to neither unity nor action.

On the contrary it was saturated with antagonism, anger and hate, a direct result of the Arlozoroff libel.

"Indeed, the atmosphere was permeated by a deliberate tendency to isolate and humiliate the Jabotinsky-led Revisionist faction," recollects Dr. Joseph B. Schechtman, who was a prominent member of the Revisionist delegation to the 18th Congress. It was at this Congress that the Socialists declared that: "there is in this hall a Party, together with which Eretz Israel Labor refuses to sit on the Presidium; this is the Party in which people who are being officially suspected of organizing the murder of one of our comrades grew up."[6] As a result, by a majority of two votes (151 to 149) the Congress accepted a motion which precluded Revisionist representation in the Presidium.

In his post mortem of the Congress, Jabotinsky wrote: "It humiliated our Nation before the arrogance of the Third Reich; broke the united front of the boycott movement and failed to unmask the anti-Zionist essence of the Mandatory Power's policy which hides under a cloak of verbal benevolence. Worst of all, it offered the world an ugly show of internecine hatred. Also, it has committed what I do not hesitate to call a crime, by intervening in a matter *sub judice* and pushing to the gallows two young Jews who claim to be innocent and whom I firmly believe to be innocent."[7]

Following the dark days of the 18th Congress, Jabotinsky and the Revisionist leaders concentrated their efforts on organizing the best possible defense for the accused *hetarim*.

Funds had to be solicited and a lawyer of high standing had to be engaged. Also, non-Jewish assistance, especially among British notables, had to be sought. Finally, the services of a well known Anglo-Jewish barrister, Horace Samuel were secured. Likewise, Col. Patterson, (of the Jewish Legion fame) agreed to "look into the matter" and intervene with the authorities.

In the meantime, more and more voices were being raised in influential circles refuting the charges against the accused. The most powerful of such voices was that of the venerable Chief Rabbi Abraham I. Kook.

Between May 16th and June 8, two verdicts were handed down by the British Court, in which Zvi Rosenblatt was acquitted while Abraham Stavsky was sentenced to death by hanging. Stavsky's defense lodged an immediate appeal. Likewise, Jabotinsky himself devoted much time approaching old friends from the Jewish Legion days, such as Wickham Steed of the "Times" of London and Herbert Sidebotham. Several prominent British politicians were induced to visit the Colonial Office and to demand guarantees for an unbiased trial.

Finally, on July 19th, Stavsky was acquitted of all charges by the Court of

Appeal.

Nevertheless, the internal emotions of hate and vengeance succeeded in poisoning the entire rank and file of the Zionist Left, which continued to wave the flag of this blood libel for many years to come.

Even today, most leftists who lived through these agonizing days may well share in the sentiments expressed by one of the young Mapai leaders of the time, Mrs. Golda Meir (Meyrson). After some 40 years since the murder of Dr. Arlozoroff, she wrote: "The identity of the assassins will probably never be known, but at the time virtually the entire leadership of the shocked and bereaved Labor Movement was convinced of Rosenblatt's and Stavsky's guilt, as I myself was. At all events, with Arlozoroff's murder, what had been for years a growing friction between the Left and the Right wings of the Zionist Movement, turned into a breach that in some respects has not healed to this day, and perhaps will never heal entirely."[8]

Historians agree that it was this blood libel that marked the beginning of the malice and hate that afflicted the normal functioning of the initially pure-spirited movement Dr. Herzel is credited with creating.

The Left wing of Zionism was proselytized into believing that Revisionism is nothing less than the devil incarnated: "The Revisionists were denounced as fascists, Ben Gurion called Jabotinsky "Vladimir Hitler" and, as far as members of Mapai were concerned, the Revisionists would not stop at murder."[9]

There are others, who do not accept the theory that the Left's anger and hate erupted following the tragic loss of their favorite son. These observers recall that Arlozoroff's murder coincided with the stark revelation of the fact that Jabotinsky's activism and the general ideology of the Revisionists had been speedily gaining in popularity among the Jewry of Europe. In fact, with the dangerous growth of Hitlerism and the gradual distancing of Britain from its obligations under the Balfour Declaration, the Revisionists were becoming a serious threat to Mapai's domination of the Zionist Organization. Already in 1931, Jabotinsky's followers garnered some 21% of the Zionist Congress' votes as compared to 29% gained by the Labor.

Many Revisionists had little doubt that Labor's fear of losing the control of the Zionist Organization matured into a collective paranoia, an obsession which helped to stimulate the unbridled denunciations leading to the blood libel in the Arlozoroff case.

It became a question of what came first, the chicken or the egg. The Left continue to believe that it was the Arlozoroff murder that triggered obsessive and permanent resentment bordering on hate. On the other hand, the nationalist element of the Zionist movement remained convinced that it was the deep ideological division, combined with a fear of losing the reins of the Movement to Jabotinsky and his followers that invigorated the latent hatred of their despised opponent.

When one looks objectively into the circumstances of this tragedy, it is indeed difficult to imagine that an accusation of murder, rejected by a foreign (British) court, could continue to poison the minds of thousands of Zionist Leftists for more than five generations. Yet the venom of hate, as revealed by this element, had neither softened nor been neutralized, even during the monstrous tragedy that befell the entire Jewish Nation. On the contrary, it progressed from the early disputes of pre-Arlozoroff days through the dark years of the Holocaust and through the recriminations that followed the assassination of Israel's Prime Minister, Itzhak Rabin.

There is no better way to study the atmosphere within the Zionist Movement at the time of the Arlozoroff case than to skip some 70 years to the present and read a scholarly opinion defining the attitude of Israel's Left of today. This opinion is offered in an article in the *Jerusalem Post* of April 9, 2004, by a former socialist, Amnon Lord: "After I started studying the nature of the Israeli "LEFT", its roots, its history, its patterns of action and its ideology, I concluded that a leftist's loyalty is almost completely to a political organization, to a Movement. It has been said about European social-democratic parties that they do not recognize the sovereignty of the state, only the sovereignty of the party. That is true of the Israeli Left too."[10]

Certainly, this atmosphere and mode of behavior could not have been triggered by the murder of one of Left's prominent leaders, which took place some generations ago. It must have come from the "genes" of the universal movement of the "Left" as inherited from Lenin's socialism of the dark days of the Russian revolution.

****

In spite of the highly emotional antagonism between Zionism's socialist and nationalist wings following the deeply wounding Arlozoroff case, both Ben Gurion and Jabotinsky realized that, in the long run, the major fatality could be Zionism itself.

Thus, during weeks of meetings and negotiations, the two leaders reached a provisional agreement which would, hopefully, lead to a certain resolution to the perennial enmity of the two opposing elements within the Zionist Organization.

However, in March of 1935, a Histadrut (Labor union) referendum took place and resolved to "reject the Ben Gurion-Jabotinsky agreement" by a margin of 15,227 to 10,187 votes. Reluctantly, Ben Gurion accepted the outcome.

Thus, the prospect of establishing some unity of purpose and normalcy of relations began to fade. By February 13, 1935, Ben Gurion announced that all efforts at reconciliation had failed and as a result, the Zionist Actions Committee decided to reject Jabotinsky's plea for a "round table conference" of all Zionist parties and condemned the Revisionists' petition for a world wide boycott of Nazi Germany. The Actions Committee also ruled to curtail the free distribution of the shekel (membership card) in favor of a new law by which membership in the Zionist Organization would be restricted to those able to purchase a shekel. And in its further attempt to hamper the Revisionists' capacity for independent action, the Actions Committee ruled to change the text of the shekel (Zionist membership ticket) obliging every voter to denounce independent Revisionist political activity.

The Revisionists, led by Jabotinsky, declared in turn, that the Party could not continue its normal functioning under such restraints, nor could it carry out its program of action towards securing a Jewish State with a Jewish majority, which was its very "raison d'etre".

Furthermore, the Revisionists accused the Jewish Agency of attempting to conduct an illegal screening of certificates to Israel, as a result of which only an infinitesimal number of *betarim* were able to enter Palestine.

Thus, on April 22, Jabotinsky addressed the Revisionist World Executive with a proposal to organize a new, independent Zionist Organization. The Executive accepted the proposal with enthusiasm and voted to submit it to a plebiscite of the Party.

On June 3, 1935 the Party plebiscite accepted the proposal by a margin of 167,000 votes to 3,000 and a New Zionist Organization was born.

****

During these turbulent days in Zionism, the fate of European Jewry was about to be sealed. Between this time and the Chamberlain surrender at Munich, the New Zionist Organization was frantically involved in an attempt to influence Britain, the USA and other European countries to open the doors of Palestine and help to promote a mass evacuation of European Jewry. This effort was met with a sharp and bitter rebuke from the "official" Zionist circles.

Again the Revisionists were condemned as irresponsible hot heads and spreaders of panic. In addressing this problem, Schechtman wrote: "One of these 'official' Zionist leaders, disparagingly declared that 'Jabotinsky never lived in the regular time of day; he had his own time: when we, Zionists, saw the clock at six, he saw it at twelve'. Meant as a reproach, this formula offers a significant clue to Jabotinsky's unique personal mission in Jewish life, he had his own time. And bitter experience has proven that he was prophetically right when he 'saw the clock at twelve' and not at six, as did the others. The symbolic difference of six hours roughly corresponds to the six million of European Jews who perished in the Holocaust."[11]

Thus, the days of Kristal Nacht find the world embracing appeasement, Britain turning away from their Balfourian obligations and world Jewry divided, confused and hideously threatened.

And while the dark clouds were converging on the skies of Europe, the Nazis in Germany spoke clearly of their aim to rid Germany of the Jews. Nevertheless, the world looked on in silence and indifference. No fleeing Jews were accepted anywhere in the world (with a notable exception of China where some 20,000 German, Austrian and Polish Jews found refuge during the years of the Holocaust).

Asked what will happen to Jews of Germany who will not manage to leave before it is harnessed to total war, an article in the SS newspaper Das Schwarze Korps. on November 24th 1938, provided the answer: "The fate of such Jews, as the outbreak of war should still find in Germany, would be their final end, their annihilation (*vernichtung*)."[12]

This was the scene in which Jewry found itself on the eve of the Second World War: Nazism threatens Europe; the world is silent and Zion . . . weeps.

The very obvious, desperate solution was to break open the gates of Palestine and to lead European Jewry into the second exodus–mass evacuation. But even this demand of Jabotinsky and his followers met with resistance, abuse and slander.

Notes

1. *My Life* by Golda Meir. Page 144
2. House of Commons. June 23, 1933
3. Report by His Majesty's Government to the Council of the League of Nations on the Administration of Palestine and Transjordan, 1934.
4. Quoted in *Our Voice*, July 1934
5. *Fighter and Prophet* by Dr. Joseph B. Schechtman, Pages 186-187
6. *Fighter and Prophet* by Dr. Joseph B. Schechtman. Page 192
7. *Fighter and Prophet* by Dr. Joseph B. Schechtman. Page 197
8. *My Life* by Golda Meir, Page 145
9. *A History of the Jews* by Paul Johnson, Page 446
10. Amnon Lord is also the author of *The Israeli Left: From Socialism to Nihilism*
11. *Fighter and Prophet* by Dr. Joseph B. Schechtman. Page 335
12. *The Final Solution* by G. Reithlinger, Page 8

Chapter 3
The Evacuation Fiasco

Most scholars of the Holocaust claim that "Kristal Nacht"—the night of the broken glass, which took place on November 9, 1938—marks the genesis of the "final solution." Of course, this is not correct. "Kristal Nacht" came about as a direct retaliation for the assassination of a German diplomat in Paris, by a young Jewish patriot—Herschel Grynszpan. Hitler's plans for wiping out Jewry, on the other hand, were clearly spelled out in his "Mein Kemf" in 1924 for the whole world to read.

Obvious preparations for the "final solution" were made in stages immediately following Hitler's take over of the Chancellery. The Draconian anti-Jewish regulations came into effect with the publication of the infamous Neurenburg Laws, on September 15, 1935. Since then, all but the blind saw, all but the deaf heard, and all but the morons knew. . . .

In spite of this, it is wrong to say that "the world" is responsible for the monstrous tragedy of the Holocaust. There is enough blame to go around; and there is no comfort in hiding it. However, it must be recorded clearly, that the perpetrators of this hideous crime were Adolf Hitler, who masterminded it, his gangster associates, who actively supported him, and a vast majority of the German citizens, who made it possible by their active and passive countenance, cruel indifference and cowardly acceptance.

There are others, notably the Government and citizens of the United States of America, who must bear responsibility for not stepping in with all their might and influence, both political and physical, in order to minimize the horrendous consequences of the "final solution". Thousands upon thousands of desperate refugees could have been rescued and absorbed before the gas ovens were even lit. Other thousands could have been saved if the United States Air Force, together with their allies, would have answered the desperate pleas of the Jewish victims to bomb the death camps and the rail system which brought them, each day, to their merciless slaughter.

But the biggest and the worst associate in the systematic annihilation of European Jewry was the Government, the media and the general public of Great Britain.

No, the British did not murder six million Jews of Europe. The Germans did. But England was the only Country on earth which could have opened the gates of Palestine, as they were obligated to by an internationally confirmed agreement, under the Mandate and the Balfour Declaration. This alone would have helped rescue more than a million Jews with nowhere to flee.

History must not fail to assign to Great Britain the full weight of responsibility for allowing millions of Jews to be liquidated by the Germans at the time when the notorious White Paper closed the gates of Palestine, during the final hours preceding the eruption of the Second World War.

At this time, the so-called democratic world was doing everything to prevent this world conflagration. The Allies were preoccupied appeasing the Germans, while the British were busy appeasing the Arabs. In the meantime, the Jews of Europe were balancing on the brink of total liquidation.

During this desperate period, the only possible solution to the Jewish plight would have been a total and immediate evacuation from Europe to Palestine. Such an evacuation would have had to be preceded by a very thorough political campaign aimed at intimidating, encouraging and forcing Britain to honor its Balfourian vows and allow the gates of Palestine to be opened completely. Likewise, with sufficient, combined pressure of world Jewry, the Government of the United States quite likely could have been persuaded to use its significant influence on Britain, to facilitate the escape of European Jewry to Palestine.

Whether these and other forms of pressure would have succeeded or not, we will never know. However, tragically and with bitterness and sorrow, we must record the fact that no such pressures were even contemplated. In fact, when Jabotinsky was clamoring for evacuation, "official" Zionists, joined by prominent public figures such as Albert Einstein and Shalom Asch, were ridiculing him and anesthetizing Jews of Europe into staying put and ignoring the "hysterical" voices of the Revisionist Zionists. In one of his most vicious attacks against Jabotinsky's evacuation plan, Shalom Asch said (as noted by Izik Remba in his book "Jabotinsky"—pages 164-166): "What Jabotinsky is now doing to Poland goes beyond all limits... One has to have a heart of stone to be devoid of any feeling for human sufferings to be so brazen as to come to Poland with such proposals at such a terrible time. . . . Heaven help a people with such leaders."*

Even among his former "Moment" colleagues, the evacuation plan received a strong rebuke from Noah Prilutzky, who stated: "Jabotinsky wants to evacuate from Poland a considerable part of her present Jewish population, and I would like to have here not three and a half but seven million Jews; this would increase our strength in fighting the anti-Semites." [1]

At this time, the official policy of the Zionist Organization was opposed to the evacuation idea, although the Labor leaders in Palestine vociferously objected to appeasing Britain on this issue.

The fiercest storm developed over Jabotinsky's approach to the Government of Poland. He firmly believed that there may be a concert of interests between Poland, which was eager to get rid of its Jews and the cause of Zionism, which aimed at ingathering all Jews in Palestine. In fact, he did find willingness to cooperate in the form of assistance in military training, procurement of boats for "illegal" immigration and the like.

The anti-evacuation campaign was not restricted to Poland. It spread to both Palestine and the United States of America.

In Tel Aviv, the Labor's mouthpiece "Davar" wrote in its editorial on October 19, 1937: "the Fuhrer Jabotinsky, all these years, had been busily disturbing every sound idea in Zionism. We Jews will not let ourselves be expelled to Palestine with the help of Polish anti-Semites."

On the other hand, the General Zionists in Palestine voiced their agreement with Jabotinsky's approach. In their daily "Ha Boker," writing on the subject of "Poland and Zionism", they simply stated, "Jabotinsky was right". This sentiment was echoed by several other leaders of Zionist and local Palestine bodies during an interview by the Revisionist group's daily "Hayarden." All firmly endorsed Jabotinsky's stand. [2]

No less contradictory was the reaction in the United States.

The late Dr. Stephen S. Wise, considered a leading figure of American Jewry immediately before and during the Second World War, became a vigorous opponent of Jabotinsky and the Revisionists. In fact, Rabbi Wise maintained a close relationship with the Left Zionists and supported their anti-evacuation position. At a conference in New York, in January 1937, Rabbi Wise characterized as "Apostates . . . Vladimir Jabotinsky and any other Jew who conducts negotiations with Colonel Beck and the Polish Government for immigration of three million (!) Jews". [3]

In reviewing the reaction of the Left to Jabotinsky's call for evacuation, one may be tempted to find it stained with duplicity. Especially so, in view of Ben Gurion's and Mapai's constant demands for more entry certificates from the British.

In reality, it was quite consistent with the Left's partisan chauvinism.

On one hand, the Zionist Leftists were eager to bring in as many pioneers to Palestine as possible. These pioneers would continue to be selected by the Jewish Agency in favor of their like-thinkers and supporters.

However, mass evacuation, as advocated by the Revisionists, would obviously dismantle the certificate system of quota allocations and "flood" Palestine with Jews of all walks of life, including members of the nationalistic front, such as the Revisionists and their youth—the Betar.

Of course, they had good reason to be apprehensive of Jewish mass immigration, especially from Poland, where adherents to Jabotinsky's beliefs were growing daily. Thus, evacuation could have spelled danger to their domination of the Jewish Agency, the Yishuv and the Zionist Organization. Surprisingly, all the continuous, hate-inspired denunciations of the New Zionist Organization did little to affect the attitude of an average Polish Jew. Among them, Jabotinsky became the symbol of redemption. "His visits to Warsaw and other towns were considered an occasion for celebration", notes Samuel Katz, one of the leading Revisionists of that period. He also observed that during such visits "Jabotinsky would find the streets and houses decorated with flags and garlands. Women and children would scatter flowers in his path. One could sense the current of pride which ran through the Jewish masses, the feeling of increased security in an insecure world, which gripped them as a result of his coming; here was that one man who could negotiate with statesmen for us on equal terms; here was that one Jew whose main concern we were, just because we were Jews". [4]

By 1939, the world seemed to have positioned itself firmly on the threshold of World War II. At this time there was some significant clamor for unity among the Yishuv and within the Zionist Organization. Jabotinsky was approached by his colleagues to seek some modus vivendi with the "Old" Zionist Organization. Likewise the World Mizrahi's prominent leader, Rabbi Ze'ev Gold, suggested creating a united front, including the Revisionists and the Group B of the General Zionists. Jabotinsky was ready to participate in serious discussions for such a union providing a preliminary conference would be held to seek mutuality of aim and purpose. No such conference ever came about. . . .

By now, the clock of history struck 12!

For Hitler, World War II was the curtain opener for the final solution. This father of evil had always insisted that, if a war came, it would be the work of the Jews, acting on the international stage; and when it did come, he held the Jews responsible for all the death that ensued. The conclusion implicit in this argument was that "the Jews had no moral right to their lives either. Indeed, he said on a number of occasions that war would precipitate a 'final solution' of the 'Jewish problem'". [5]

Even in the concept of Nazism, war created a state of urgency for the implementation of Hitler's "final solution". A contemporary historian, Paul Johnson observed in his important work—"History of the Jews", that for Hitler "war brought its own exigencies, and it also drew a veil over many activities. It was the necessary context in which genocide could be committed. So far from the Jews creating the war, then, it was rather Hitler who willed the war in order to destroy the Jews".[6]

For Jabotinsky there was little he could do during the "phony" phase of the war, within the confines of Europe. His obvious frontier for action now lay over the ocean—in the United States of America. It was here that he should be championing the cause of unlimited Jewish immigration for all escapees from Hitler's hell. Likewise, it was in America that he had to influence the Government in favor of creating a Jewish armed contingent which could participate in war against Hitler and in exerting pressure on Britain to stand by its long abandoned commitments for an independent Jewish State.

Jabotinsky was familiar with America from his previous visits. He knew well that Zionism was accepted reluctantly and luke warmly by the average American Jew. He was also well aware of the initially anti-Zionist stand taken by the popular Reform Movement and the close ties of local Jewish leaders with the Old Zionist Organization, its Leftist leadership and its Palestinian arm—the Vaad Leumi.

And yet, Jabotinsky and his associates in America were all pleasantly surprised to observe how many Americans—Jews and Gentiles alike—grew to understand him better, appreciate him more and even accept his monistic nationalism—favorably.

In July 1940, the Sagall brothers, both non-Revisionist admirers of Jabotinsky, made an effort to consolidate the Zionist fractions regarding the creation of a Jewish Army. Both brothers had extensive connections with leading members of the Zionist Organization in Britain as well as with non-Jewish friends of the Zionist cause. On July 2, 1940; they organized a luncheon. Besides Jewish leaders like Chaim Weizmann and Israel Zief, they invited such dignitaries as: Sir Gothbert Haslam, M.P., Colonel Charles Ponsonby (Permanent Parliamentary Secretary of the British Foreign Minister, Anthony Eden), Sir Maurice Bonham (prominent leader of the Liberal Party) and Sir Hugh Seely (Under Secretary for Air). Asked about his attitude towards the idea of the Jewish Army and towards Jabotinsky's action in this field, Dr. Weizmann explained that he too was in favor of the Jewish Army. He added that there were essential differences between Jabotinsky and himself in internal Zionist matters: Jabotinsky wanted a Jewish State immediately, while he, Weizmann, was a man who believed in slow methods, such as immigrating into Palestine at the rate of several thousand a year. However he thought that cooperation with Jabotinsky on the issue of the Jewish Army was not impossible. In fact, he suggested that during his forthcoming visit to America, he planned to get in touch with him.

In the wake of this luncheon, Zief arranged a meeting on July 5, between Weizmann and Robert Briscoe, member of the New Zionist Organization, who was also a deputy of the Irish Parliament. According to Briscoe, Weizmann reconfirmed his "full sympathy with the Jewish Army project and his plan to meet with Jabotinsky in America." To avoid a misunderstanding, a text of a cable to this effect was drafted: Before sending the cable to the New Zionist Organization in New York, apprising them of the basic understanding reached with Dr. Weizmann, Briscoe send the draft of the cable for Weizmann's confirmation.

When Weizmann was shown the draft, he postponed signing it from one day to another. Finally, he admitted that he could not sign the cable before clearing it with the Executive of the Jewish Agency. After several other delays, Dr. Weizmann abruptly reversed his earlier stand on the matter.

Mr. A. Abrahams, Political Secretary of the New Zionist Organization, informed Colonel Amery, an old friend of Jabotinsky, of these developments. As a result, Amery wrote to Weizmann expressing concern. In his reply, Weizmann stated: "I am sorry that you should have been worried by Mr. Abrahams—and in a matter of so little importance. I did not promise that I would send a cable to Mr. Jabotinsky in support of his scheme, since I know nothing about such a scheme. Nor would I care to be mixed up in any of his activities, in America or elsewhere". [7]

As a direct consequence of this inexplicable turn about by Weizmann, the

New Zionist Organization's organ "The Jewish Standard" announced the breakdown of the attempts to reach any agreement, while Jabotinsky told the Sagall brothers that ". . . while appreciating your friendly efforts, I am compelled to consider the Agency's failure to answer direct, as conclusively discouraging any positive anticipation; whatever further initiative shall be left entirely to the Agency". [8]

In spite of these and other setbacks, Jabotinsky continued his endless efforts to establish some form of unity among Zionists, as a whole. He believed in an urgent necessity to establish a Jewish National Committee, the absence of which stood in the way of an irresistibly powerful campaign for a Jewish Army. He pleaded with his opponents of the Left that this is no time for ideological warfare between Jews—it was time for unity and combined action. In fact, Jabotinsky, according to his close associates Remba, Abrahams and Schechtman, was ready and willing to make all imaginable concessions, to sink all differences, believing that once Jewish leaders stood shoulder to shoulder in the common struggle for the Jewish Army, all else would follow.

Tragically, this was not to be. All his efforts to move the World Zionist Organization proved completely fruitless. As noted by Dr. S. Magoshes of "Der Tag": "His proffered hand was rejected. I know because I tried to mediate between Jabotinsky and the World Zionist leaders. Stephen S. Wise would not hear of any conversation with Jabotinsky, nor would Chaim Weizmann". [9]

It was now summer of 1940. Discouraged and fatigued, Jabotinsky continued to pursue his efforts to establish Jewish unity, a Jewish Army and a combined, all-Zionist front for the establishment of a Jewish State.

Never before was Jabotinsky known to complain about being tired. By now he voiced such complaints frequently and to many of his friends and colleagues. Possibly with an aim of relieving the daily pressures, it was suggested that Jabotinsky pay a visit to the Betar summer camp, located at the outskirts of New York. Jabotinsky was overjoyed at the prospect of spending a weekend among his Betarim.

Shortly before reaching the camp, Jabotinsky showed signs of utter exhaustion. He was accompanied by several friends, among whom was A. Hanin[†], the current leader of the American Betar and an intimate friend of this author. According to Hanin, Jabotinsky was in pain. He reviewed the Betar guard of honor briefly and requested to be given a few minutes to rest in bed. But the obvious heart attack developed unabated and the sudden end came at 10:45 p.m.

As the word passed from mouth to mouth, from city to city and from continent to continent, the stunned, orphaned Jewish world submerged into deep mourning. The universal reaction to Jabotinsky's death betrayed the overwhelming love, respect and admiration he won among the Jewish masses from China to Palestine and from Europe to America.

Jews, lingering in Nazi concentration camps, risked their lives to recite the Kaddish, exchange reminiscences and bow their heads in prolonged silence.

Zeev (Vladimir) Jabotinsky was buried in New Montefiore Cemetery in Farmingdale, Long Island, New York. Thousands lined the route of the funeral cortege. There were no speeches, no eulogies at the burial. Only a chorus of one hundred and fifty cantors took part in the funeral rites. . . .

Jabotinsky's remains were not brought to Palestine in spite of the fact that, in all likelihood, the British Government would not voice any objections. They were afraid of Jabotinsky alive. Towards Jabotinsky—dead, they could afford to show their British sense of compassion.

Not so with his Leftist opponents in the World Zionist Organization.

In his last will, Jabotinsky left instructions to be buried "wherever I happen to die; and my remains (should I be buried outside Palestine) may not be transferred to Palestine unless by order of that Country's eventual Jewish Government".

Throughout the years of holding the premiership of Israel, Ben Gurion refused to issue such an order. When asked, point blank, by Jabotinsky's biographer Dr. B. Schechtman "Why does the Government of Israel, of which you are the head, not give such an order?", Ben Gurion replied (on October 3, 1956 that in his view "only the remains of Theodore Herzel and of Baron Edmund de Rothschild ought to be reburied in Israel; as for others—Israel needs live Jews, not dead ones". [10]

Notes

* At a press conference in Jerusalem, Asch repentantly said: "I deeply regret that I had fought against Jabotinsky's evacuation plan." (Herut Daily. May 5, 1952)

† Arosha Hanin originally came to the States from Harbin, China. He died in 1999 in San Francisco, California

1. *Fighter and Prophet* by Dr. Schechtman. Page 340
2. *Fighter and Prophet* by Dr. Schechtman. Page 340
3. *Jewish Daily News Bulletin*, New York, February 13, 1937
4. *Jabotinsky in Poland* by Samuel Katz, in *Zionews* Sept. 1, 1942.
5. *A History of the Jews* by Paul Johnson. Page 489
6. *A History of the Jews* by Paul Johnson. Page 489
7. Preceding three paragraphs are based on Dr. Schechtman's recollections as they appear in his *Fighter and Prophet*. Pages 393-394.
8. Cable to J. Sagall, July 31, 1940
9. *Fighter and Prophet* by Dr. Schechtman. Page 392
10. *Fighter and Prophet* by J. Schechtman. Page 401

Chapter 4
American Jewry During the Holocaust

After the death of their inspired leader, the Revisionists of the New Zionist Organization suddenly became both orphaned and languid. They continued with the motion of existence but lacked the initiative, the drive and the will.

On the other hand, the "official" Zionism in America was in the hands of attractive personalities such as Rabbis Abba Silver and Stephen Wise, and the Supreme Court Justice—Louis Brandeis, all of whom were well known and highly respected among the wide circles of the Jewish Community as well as within the corridors of power, including the White House and the Congress.

These recognized leaders of Jewry, following the example of their role models such as Weizmann's liberals in London and Zionist socialists in Palestine, accepted the Anglo-American prescription for Jews of the day: Salvation only with Allied victory!

Thus, the important and powerful Jewry of America lay almost prostrated in the midst of the process of complete annihilation of their brethren in Europe.

It was in this atmosphere of pitiful absence of leadership that Jabotinsky's young disciples—his *betarim*— and members of the Palestinian Hebrew underground, the Irgun Zvai Leumi, took matters in their own hands in order to continue the legacy of their beloved leader.

It was in the context of Jabotinsky's campaign for the Jewish Army that the Irgun delegation in America decided to pursue the course with renewed zealousness and motivation. The group included Irgun and Betar veterans such as Uda Ben Ami, Arie Ben Eliezer, Hillel Kook and Jabotinsky's son Eri. All contributed to the day and night efforts which eventually resulted in the formation of Jewish battalions fighting in the ranks of the British army to protect Palestine and to confront the Axis forces in Africa and the Middle East.

But the campaign for the Jewish Army was a long and a bitter one and, while many prominent Gentiles were eager to help with their time, talent and effort, the "official" leaders of American Jewry, together with their Left Zionist colleagues, were doing their utmost to sabotage these efforts, using the odious methods of intrigue, threats and intimidation.

As the news of the Holocaust, with all its gruesome details, began to penetrate the American media, the Committee for the Jewish Army gave way to "The Emergency Committee to Save the Jewish People of Europe." Although it replaced the Committee for the Jewish Army as the primary vehicle for the Bergson's Group, it did not abandon the project, which gradually fell into the hands of the Zionist Organization in London.

By 1943 it became obvious to the Jewish masses in America that rescuing the remnants of the slaughtered Jewry of Europe is the top priority and all efforts should be directed towards its implementation. However, the mainstream Jewish leaders in America failed to follow this popular conclusion.

In their seemingly inexplicable opposition to Bergson*, mainstream Jewish leaders were driven by their concern that the "dissidents" might begin to usurp their position as the spokesmen for American Zionism. According to Bergson's deputy, Samuel Merlin, "Stephen Wise will not tolerate any other Jewish Organization working for Palestine and stealing honors and publicity from him".[1]

Not all Zionist Organizations were as enthusiastic in their opposition to the Irgunists as the titular leaders. By 1941, the women's Zionist organization "Hadassah" was praising the Bergson Group for having "brought in new ideas and taken initiative," while the executive committee of the Zionist Organization of America acknowledged that "there seems to be a sentiment in the country in favor of coming to terms with the Jewish Army Committee." Even Nahum Goldmann of the World Jewish Congress, who would soon emerge as one of Bergson's most passionate opponents, noted "the growing strength of the Jewish Army Committee and the participation of many Zionists and important local persons in the public meetings and dinners held under its auspices." At the urging of Hadassah, the ZOA and Goldman, the leadership of the Emergency Committee for Zionist Affairs initiated merger talks with Bergson, but insisted on the right to appoint a majority of the Army Group's board members. Bergson's compromise offer of fifty percent of the seats was rejected and the talks ended unsuccessfully. [2]

In the meantime, Bergson's Group succeeded in enlisting enthusiastic cooperation and support from well-known and talented people who were previously unrelated to the cause of Zionism. Among these stood out the popular and successful writer and producer—Ben Hecht.

In their aggressive attempts to rescue the remnants of European Jewry, the Bergson group also befriended senators, congressmen and members of the Administration. They achieved remarkable success through publications of full page ads in prominent newspapers around the country. At one point, Ben Hecht helped them organize and write a powerful pageant: "We will Never Die." This, along with other successful ventures on behalf of attempts to rescue European Jewry, was crudely and viciously sabotaged by Rabbi Wise and his followers.

The opposition reached unacceptable proportions when it resorted to intimidation and was accompanied by intrigue, rumor-mongering and slander.

Another well known personality to join the Bergson Group's efforts was Will Rogers, Jr.*, son of the famous humorist. Rogers recalled that "the most effective technique of all the methods we used was the ads... They were hard-hitting and they had simple typography... They carried tremendous impact... I can remember when they appeared in the paper even around the halls of Congress. there was conversation... I would go down to the floor of Congress and they would be talking about it... 'Look at this' or, 'Isn't this outrageous?' or. 'Shouldn't something be done?' Very effective. Very effective". [3]

Another prominent collaborator with the Bergson Group was a famous Jewish journalist—Max Lerner.[†] In an interview with Martin Ostrow, as late as March 5, 1992, Max Lerner recalled: "By 1943 I fully realized that the story of the 'Final Solution' is being white-washed by the establishment press. I have asked myself why? It was a big story...One answer is the hypersensitivity of the New York Times, because of its Jewish ownership, to the question of how it treated news affecting the Jews and their rescue...A good newspaperman, no matter how skeptical he may be when he sees a dramatic story is bound to react to it with a sense of 'I would like to be the first ready to deal with this; I would like to get a scoop on it; I would like to have my name associated with this'. But there were no newspapermen at that time who really felt that way. It's interesting that the great columnists, for example someone like Walter Lippmann. who responded to every important world event with great eloquence and great learning. Lippmann did not respond to this. Lippmann was a Jew, a self-hating Jew who wanted to hide his Jewish origins.

"So that between someone like Lippmann and the whole sensitivity of newspapers to charges of being too influenced by Jews, put all of these together and you get the answer of the dismal cloak of ignorance that was thrown over the whole story."

"But the real news about what was happening did not come really through the newspapers. It came through the dramatic ads which our committee, the Bergson committee (as written by Ben Hecht) which appeared in the newspapers. that is where most people really began to learn what the truth of it was and I was happy to be part of the effort for them to learn the truth". [4]

It is nothing short of amazing to learn that these and many other non-partisan souls. who volunteered to give of themselves for a real humanitarian cause. became objects of harassment and intimidation.

Ben Hecht's dramatic pageant "We will never Die" opened on March 9. Hecht recruited prominent actors for the pageant's cast which included Paul Muni. Edward G. Robinson and Stella Adler. Billy Rose was the producer and Moss Hart—the director. In three acts the pageant portrayed Jewry's contribution to civilization and detailed the program of Nazi massacre. Forty thousand people flocked to see the pageant during its two performances at Madison Square Garden in New York. Following this amazing success, "We Will Never Die" was staged again, this time in Washington D.C.'s Constitution Hall. Among the audiences set as guest of honor, the first lady—Eleanor Roosevelt. hundreds of congressmen, cabinet members and Supreme Court justices. as well as members of the international diplomatic corps. The pageant was successfully repeated to full houses in Philadelphia, Chicago, Boston and

Los Angeles.

But the snowballing success of "We Will Never Die" pageant brought in its wake a more organized and bitterer opposition. In fact obstruction became a more serious problem than mere non-cooperation. "We Will Never Die" developed into a setting for a major conflict between established Jewish groups and the Bergsonites, concerning the plight of European Jewry. Wyman, in his book "Abandonment" recalls: "About six weeks before the Madison Square Garden premier, Hecht, hoping to obtain broad sponsorship of the event, organized a meeting of representatives of Jewish organizations to unveil the project. Bergson told the meeting he would refrain from using the Army Committee's name in connection with the pageant if the other organizations would agree to sponsor it. But festering intracommunal tensions proved too onerous to achieve Hecht's goal; the gathering dissolved in acrimony and insults between rival groups". [5]

Based on a report stored at the Yale University Library, Palestine Statehood Committee Papers, Box 13, dated "1944," it is recorded that through the intervention of the American Jewish Congress and the Zionist Organization of America, performances of "We Will Never Die" were cancelled in Kingston, Rochester, Buffalo, Baltimore, Gary and Pittsburgh. In a typical case of such a cancellation, the report relates how in Baltimore. Rabbi A.I. Rosenberg succeeded in organizing a luncheon for the purpose of creating a local sponsor committee to present "We Will Never Die." There was considerable enthusiasm among prominent town's people. The Mayor of Baltimore promised to preside at the luncheon. "But the Community Council there, on orders from New York, engaged in a bitter fight against the organizers, using all means of calumny, slander, smearing of the Emergency Committee, its members and Mr. Ben Ami personally. The Community Council, under its executive director, Mr. Leon Sachs, organized a 'telephone campaign', calling every single person liable to help the pageant and attempting to influence them not to come to the luncheon. As a result, a few hours before the luncheon the Mayor decided not to attend". [6]

In other cities, local sponsors of the show were said to have been told that the pageant was the handiwork of irresponsible extremists who were undermining the established Jewish leadership.

According to some accounts, Stephen Wise had even urged New York Governor Thomas Dewey to cancel plans to declare March 9, the date of the show's Madison Square Garden debut, an official day of mourning for European Jewry. [7]

This campaign was not only directed against the pageant. Its main purpose was to intimidate and eventually to silence the voice of activism as represented by the Bergson Group and their many followers. Typically, the benefits to the overall cause of Zionism were readily compromised.

The "official" Jewish leadership in the Community as well as within the context of "official Zionism" was primarily concerned with personal and organizational self-preservation as the "only" true representatives of the Jewish Community and Zionism combined.

In his work "Race Against Death," David Wyman observed: "If Bergson's success stimulated some Jewish leaders to consider cooperating with him, it provoked others to look for ways to undermine him. Stephen Wise, together with Nahum Goldmann of the World Jewish Congress, vigorously denounced Bergson during a meeting with Breckinridge Long (assistant secretary in charge of refugee matters and a prominent anti-Semite) on October 6, 1943. Bergson's success had stimulated those Jewish leaders' fears that the dissidents were usurping the established leadership, and they labored to impress upon government officials that Bergson did not represent American Jewish opinion. Their solution: Either draft Bergson or deport him. Officials at both the Justice Department and the State Department explored the suggestions but ultimately advised that making a 'martyr' out of Bergson would be worse than leaving him alone". [8]

Ignoring all efforts to cow them into irreverence, Bergson's "Emergency Committee to Save the Jewish People of Europe" continued its work by approaching and influencing prominent Congressmen and Administration officials to pass a resolution in favor of establishing a War Refugee Board, which would be empowered by the President to deal directly with the issue of rescuing the remnants of European Jewry. In this, they were finally successful and the resolution they introduced, passed the Senate with almost no obstruction.

Secretary of the Treasury Henry Morgenthau, who was deeply involved in pushing for the adoption of the Refugee Resolution, recalls in his diaries: "The tide was running with me... The fact that the resolution passed the Senate, convinced the President to really act on establishing the War Refugee Board. I think those six months before (the Rescue Resolution) I couldn't have done it". [9]

Likewise, the *Christian Science Monitor* reported that "the establishment of the War Refugee Committee is the outcome of pressure brought to bear by the Emergency Committee to Save the Jewish People of Europe—a group made up of both Jews and non-Jews that has been active in the capital in recent months". [10]

Even the *Washington Post* noted that "in view of Bergson's industrious spadework on behalf of rescue, the Emergency Committee was entitled to take credit for the President's forehanded move. Bergson had emerged as a political force, playing a central role in bringing about the Roosevelt Administration's most significant response to Hitler's annihilation of the Jews". [11]

Sen. Guy Gillette, another dedicated friend of Zionism, candidly discussed the obstruction that he encountered from Zionist leaders, when attempting to push for the message of the Refugee Committee resolution: "These people used every effort, every means at their disposal to block the resolution. They tried to defeat it by offering changes, insisting on an amendment to it that would raise the question of Zionism or anti-Zionism...or anything that might stop and block the action that we were seeking... I wish these damned Jews would make up their minds what they want. I could not get inside the committee room without being buttonholed out here in the corridor by representatives who said that the Jewish people of America did not want the passage of this resolution". [12]

Chapter 4

No attempt to coordinate the activity of rescuing Jews from Europe would meet with positive reaction from the "official" leaders of American Jewry. Instead, precious time was wasted on intrigue and obstruction.

While news began to spell out more and more of the horrors of the "final solution", the only active reaction seemed to come from the heirs of Jabotinsky, in the form of Bergson's various committees. They were generously and loyally supported by thousands of Jews and Gentiles who contributed money and time to bring the message of urgency to the Government and the Congress of the United States of America.

Not surprisingly, the elements opposed to activism of the Bergson Group found ready and willing allies in the persons of known anti-Zionists. Some of these politicians were Jews from an organization known as the "American Jewish Committee." The well recognized villain of such self-hating Jews was, without doubt, a man President Roosevelt chose to be his advisor and guide on Jewish affairs—Mr. Samuel Rosenman. Rosenman was an attorney who became justice of the New York State Supreme Court and eventually—President Roosevelt's senior speechwriter as well as his closest adviser on Jewish affairs.

Not surprisingly, Rosenman was a leading member of the American Jewish Committee. Often he counseled FDR to ignore requests from Jewish organizations for steps such as increasing refugee immigration to the United States, pressing Britain on its Palestine policy, or taking measures to rescue Jews from Hitler. It was Rosenman who persuaded Roosevelt to refrain from meeting representatives of the four hundred rabbis whom the Bergson Group brought to Washington, in October 1943. [13]

Among the Morgenthau Diaries, there are documents revealing the "tragic history of this Government's handling of the 'final solution' matter". This report also indicates that "certain State Department officials are guilty not only of gross procrastination and willful failure to act, but even of willful attempts to prevent action from being taken to rescue Jews from Hitler".

Tragically, the Jewish Community of America must look back and point out that its leadership, along with the leadership of the "Official" Zionist Organization, if already dead—must be turning in their graves. And if alive, they must be riddled with a very guilty conscience...

****

By the middle of April 1943, and while the leadership of American Jewry was fiddling with petty internal strifes on issues of questionable significance, European Jewry was all but slaughtered out of existence. Almost six million Jews were being gassed, starved, shot and tortured to death without resistance, without hope and without a trace of assistance.

Only in the sewers and ruins of the Warsaw Ghetto, young men of the Socialist youth and young men of Betar, decided to go out fighting. Theirs would be a struggle for death with honor— a heroic challenge to the prime evil of mankind.

But even in this struggle, they were afflicted by the syndrome of disunity. Even in the shadows of the Warsaw Ghetto—they fought not only alone, but also ... divided!

Notes

* Peter Bergson became the pseudonym for Hillel Kook, the leading member of the Irgun delegation in America. He was the nephew of Palestine's Chief Rabbi Kook and the main initiator of the Committee to Save the Jewish People of Europe.

* Will Rogers, Jr., Democrat of California served in the US House of Representatives from 1943 to 1944.

† Max Lerner was a prominent voice of American journalism for nearly half a century. He was the author of numerous books and articles about contemporary affairs and ideas, as well as a syndicated columnist for the New York Post from 1949 to 1992.

1. *A Race Against Death* by David S. Wyman. Page 27
2. *Hadassah Minutes*, Jan. 14, 1942 and Jan. 26, 1942
3. *A Race Against Death* by Wyman. Page 74
4. Interview of Max Lerner by Martin Osraw. March 5, 1992. New York City.
5. *Abandonment* by David S. Wyman. Page 90
6. *A Race Against Death* by Wyman. Page 208
7. The charge was made in the column *Rumor Behind the News*, Hamigdal III.4 April 1943
8. *A Race Against Death* by Wyman. Pages 42-43
9. *Morgenthau Diaries* Book 710, Page 194
10. *Christian Science Monitor*. Jan 24, 1944
11. *Washington Post*. Jan 25, 1944
12. *A Race Against Death* by David Wyman. Page 146
13. *Off the Record with FDR 1942-1945*. New Brunswick, N.J. 1958, Page 209

Chapter 5
Divided They Stood

When night descended on Europe, a death sentence was passed on its Jewry. There was no escape left for the millions who could have fled, who should have been rescued and who, nevertheless, blindly followed their leaders to the abyss of the Holocaust.

This in itself is enough to condemn the world for mass murder and the "official" leadership of European Jewry for criminal neglect and nefarious dereliction of duty.

The warnings and pleas of Jabotinsky to help bring about the evacuation of Europe fell on deaf ears. They should have provided cause enough for a total reversal of the Left's partisan stand which was entrenched in deep ideological divisiveness and hate.

But the Left learned nothing. Having accepted the theory that the Jewish problem will find its solution with the final victory of the Allies, they withdrew into their routine of blindness and neglect.

In the meantime, Poland was divided between the Germans and the Russians with most of the Jewish communities falling under the shadow of the swastika. In Warsaw, where Jews were immediately segregated into a ghetto, some one million men, women and children became isolated from the rest of the world. Some succeeded in escaping into the Russian section, others attempted to hide in villages and farms. However, the bulk of Warsaw Jewry found itself locked into several blocks of streets, surrounded with barricades and concrete walls. The Jews were left with no means to earn a livelihood or care for the welfare of their families.

But this was only the beginning.

Eventually, the German conquerors began their regular "aktions". This meant selecting a quota of between 5,000 to 7,000 Jews, gathering them in a large square—the "Umschlagsplatz," then marching them off to the "Transferstelle"* where they were made to board the waiting railway wagons destined for the Treblinka and Maidanek death camps for final extermination.

Chapter 5

Only after two years of continuous "aktions" did the Left element in the ghetto realize that the entire Jewish community of Warsaw is destined for elimination. Consequently, they decided to form a resistance force called ZOB (Jewish Fighting Organization) under the command of Mordechai Anilevich. This happened in July 1942. Until then, the Left Zionists, together with the Bund, refused to entertain the notion of a rebellion against the Nazi beast in spite of the continuous and desperate urging by Jabotinsky's followers in the ghetto.

In fact, this nationalistic element, comprised of Betarim, the Revisionists and the non-affiliated, combined forces as early as 1940 (during the first days of the ghetto's existence) to form an underground organization called ZZW (Jewish Military Organization) to prepare themselves for an eventual revolt against the Nazis. The leader of this organization was David Mordechai Appelbaum, who was assisted by two other Betarim—Pawel Frankel and Leon Leib Rodal.

During the initial "actions," the ZZW organized itself and established a liaison with a prominent group of Gentile underground fighters, who were led by Captain Iwansky, better known by his nom de gare—"Bystry." ZZW acquired weapons, trained and distributed leaflets throughout the ghetto. In these leaflets they warned the Jews against assembling at the "Umschlagsplatz" and urged them to prepare for a rebellion. One of such posters survived and became a treasured possession of Chaim Lazar, himself a Polish *betari* and author of a book called "Muranowska 7" which describes in detail the role played by Betar in the Warsaw ghetto uprising. Below we reprint the contents of the poster verbatim:

BROTHERS, LET US NOT GO LIKE SHEEP TO THE SLAUGHTER!
WHOEVER ENTERS A FREIGHT CAR IS LOST FOR EVER!
THE CHANCES OF ESCAPING ARE SMALL:
THAT IS WHY WE REMAIN HERE TO FIGHT.
LET EVERY HOUSE BECOME A FORTRESS!
THE STRUGGLE FOR FREEDOM IS OUR PRIMARY AIM.

At a January 1940 meeting with ZZW commanders and a group of Polish partisans "Bystry" contributed 29 Weiss pistols from his arms store on hospital grounds, to the Jewish fighters. This marked the beginning of a close bond between the Polish resistance and the first Jewish underground organization in Warsaw. In his memoirs "Bystry" recalls: "Appelbaum was a fighting man, a true soldier in every fiber. I once spoke to him quite candidly. 'Maitek' (his nick-name) I said, 'I must confess I never expected to find such a brave soldier as you among the Jews'. 'I am the pupil of a great Jew, Ze'ev Jabotinsky, he answered. 'He taught us all to be good soldiers. There were once many like me in Poland. I am sure that in the free world there are still tens of thousands like me, and even better than me'." [1]

Between 1940 and 1941 several *"aktions"* took place. Jews, duped by their "official" representatives known in the ghetto as the "Judenrat", continued to voluntarily assemble at the Umschlagsplatz, on to the deportation station and finally—to the death camps for "final solution".

It was in the spring of 1942 that David Appelbaum received word that the Jews who were deported to the East, were being liquidated in the incinerators of the extermination camps and that the beasts were planning the mass extermination of the Warsaw ghetto. The chairman of the Judenrat, Mr. Czerniakow, upon hearing of this horrible crime that was being planned, proceeded to deny that Jews were going to be deported. And this was in June 1942! [2]

By July 23 Czerniakow was ordered to increase the next day's quota to seven thousand and to ten thousand, the next day after, which was a Shabbat. Finally, the situation became clear even to him. Left alone at his desk, he called his secretary to go out and bring him a glass of water. When she came back she found him slumped over his desk, dead. [3]

Only now, when tens of thousands of ghetto inmates were deported to death camps during the month of July 1942, did the Left realize what is in store and began to organize their own resistance organization, called the ZOB.

Of course, no such organization was needed. It would have been not only sufficient but also highly productive, if instead, the Left would have heeded ZZW's repeated pleas to join forces and form a united resistance organization. Tragically, no amount of persuasion sufficed to convince the Zionist leftists, who were ready to join forces with the anti-Zionist Bund, rather than to unite under joint command with the followers and disciples of Zeev Jabotinsky. "The ostracism of the Jabotinsky Movement and all connected with it was pursued in the ghetto as well, whether as a declared policy or unofficially," commented Chaim Lazar in his book "Muranowska 7".

Not only did the Left refuse to unite with the nationalists in their mutual struggle against the enemy, but also, they tried to eliminate from history any recording of participation in this struggle of their despised ideological opponents.

The pettiness, the dishonesty and the manipulative designs of the Left were best revealed by professor Bernard Mark, in his book "The Struggle and Destruction of the Warsaw Ghetto", published by the Polish Ministry of Defense in Warsaw in 1959. Here, he quotes verbatim a long report sent from Warsaw on the 24th of May 1944, by the Jewish National Council of Poland addressed to their superiors in London:

> "In the interests of truth we wish to deal with a number of points. On the strength of information we have received from abroad, it would appear that the Bund abroad wishes to take the credit for the fighting in Warsaw; if not all of it, at least for most of it. We wish to inform you, in the most definite manner, that this is not in accordance with the truth. For the sake of historical truth you must eradicate what is an unfounded and unjust legend. The struggle in the Warsaw ghetto, as in other ghettos and

camps, was initiated and waged by us and our affiliated organizations, first and foremost by the workers' associations and youth organizations affiliated to the Eretz Israel Labor Movement, Hehalutz, Dror, Young Hehalutz, Poalei-Zion Youth, Hashomer Hatzair, Poalei Zion and Left-wing Poalei Zion. It was these organizations that conducted and waged the battles, provided the overwhelming majority of combatants and sacrificed the greatest number of lives. The commander of the Jewish Fighting Organization was our heroic comrade, Mordechai Anilewicz, the Hashomer Hatzair leader. We had four representatives in the H.Q. Command, while the Bund had only one. Of the twenty-two fighting units, our organizations provided eighteen, the Bund—four. Bundists accounted for no more than 18% of the total number of fighting men. True, the Bund units which fought within the frame of the Jewish Fighting Organization did so as courageously as did all the other units, without exception, but it was not they that determined the prevailing atmosphere, or the course of the fighting. It is our membership who still stands at the head of the Jewish Fighting Organization.

"We were (therefore) highly astonished when the "Virtuti" Military Medal (the highest Polish military decoration) was awarded only to Michael Klapfisz, a Bund member. Klapfisz had fought bravely, but so had hundreds of other heroic fighters. If the intention was to make a symbolic award to the Jewish Fighting Organization, or to the whole body of heroic fighters, we feel that this decoration should rightfully have been awarded to the commander of the Jewish Fighting Organization, at least. We are especially pained by the fact—though we may be wrong—that the Bund has virtually monopolized the propaganda disseminated among workers' organizations abroad, especially in England and the United States, and has won over the Jewish Workers' Council in America. Do not the Right-and Left-wing Poalei Zion Parties pursue the necessary information activities in these labor circles? The labor movement all over the world should know, that it was the Zionist Labor organizations that organized and headed the Warsaw Ghetto Revolt, and that the hundreds of fighters that took part and fell in the struggle did so imbued with the firm conviction that their death would serve as a foundation for the socialist future of the Jewish masses in Eretz Israel.

—Signed by: Dr. A. Berman-Borowski, Yitzhak Zuckerman, Adv. Shimon Gottesman, Daniel Kaftor Joint and Josef Sak."

In his book the well known historian, Prof. Bernard Mark alludes to this report in the following terms: "The records of the underground movement contain a whole series of facts and items of information including, inter alia, a copy of a report drawn up by the ZOB Command and other active participants, with the help of Yitzhak Zuckerman (Antek). This report is one of the basic documents which may shed light on the period and on the Warsaw Ghetto Rising. But this report is not devoid of a certain degree of one-sidedness, and above all in regard to the other fighting organization inside the ghetto—I refer to the Jewish Military Organization." [4]

It transpired therefore that the seekers of "historical truth" were interested in such truth only insofar as it affected their organization, their Party and their members. The moment they felt themselves to be treated unfairly, they raised an outcry and appealed to the conscience of the world. Regretfully, their own conscience did not bother them enough in order to reveal the whole truth behind the epic struggle of the Warsaw Ghetto.

However, in spite of the unrelenting, bitter conflict between the opposing elements of Zionism, the Jewish soul and the Jewish spirit often find a way to overcome prejudices and inhibitions, whether social or ideological, and finally—prevail.

So it was during the days and nights of ferocious combat between the forces of evil and the naked and starving fighters of Zion.

As testified by "Bystry" and his group of Polish combatants who fought side by side with the ZZW one reads of tales of remarkable feats of bravery and courage, mutual assistance and brotherly emotions, as was often displayed between the opposing underground organizations, which together comprised the wondrous Warsaw Ghetto Resistance.

With the approach of spring in 1943, time was nearing for the final days of the Warsaw Ghetto. Through their Polish contacts among the partisans, the ZZW commanders learned of the impending diabolical scheme of the German beast—the complete liquidation (also called *"aktion"*) of the Warsaw Ghetto. Immediately they contacted the leadership of the ZOB and informed them of the German plan, thus giving them an opportunity to prepare for the battle ahead. It now appeared that coordination was finally established between the ZOB and the ZZW at this twelfth hour of the Ghetto.

The "aktion" for the liquidation of the ghetto was to be supervised by the Nazi General Jurgen Stroop, who was in the habit of issuing systematic and daily reports on how the *"aktion"* was proceeding. It is from these reports that we were able to draw the following picture of the uneven combat.

On April 19, 1943 at 6 A.M., General Stroop instructed Col. von Sammern to proceed to carry out the *"aktion"*.

The Germans penetrated into the ghetto from Nalawki and Zamenhof streets. As soon as they reached the corner of Zamenhof-Mila, they were greeted with a hail of rifle and pistol fire, hand-grenades and Molotov cocktails.

Within minutes, a deafening rumble was heard and a tank and two half-tracks advanced on the Jewish positions. However, they were unable to break through to clear the path for the SS troops that waited in the rear. Molotov bottles tossed by the Jewish fighters set the tank on fire and the two half-tracks were forced to beat a hurried retreat. By this time the Germans began to suffer casualties.

According to the first report of General Stroop: "At approximately 7:30 hours, von Sammern reported to me at my quarters and informed me that all in the ghetto was lost, that the forces he had detailed for the operation had retreated, and that there were dead and wounded—I do not recall how many". [5]

These battles were also recounted by a living witness—Dr. R. Walewski, a Revisionist member of the ZZW who gave the following account: "Muranowska Square and the adjoining buildings were closely defended by a chain of ZZW units. All through the fighting we were in constant touch with the Aryan side, from where we obtained a heavy machine-gun. This, we set up in a building on Muranowska Square, giving us control of the whole square and its approaches. Although this was the only machine-gun in the ghetto, it was able to stem the advance of the powerful Nazi forces operating in this sector. In spite of their repeated onslaughts with tanks and automatic weapons, they were unable to capture our positions. In fact, we frequently launched a counter-offensive, capturing the enemy's weapons, destroying their material and inflicting serious losses in dead and wounded." [6]

By the fifth day of the ghetto revolt, the struggle continued. It was now April 23. "Glos Warszawa" (The Voice of Warsaw) wrote in its issue No. 29, from London: "The Warsaw ghetto had for months been preparing the revolt. . . The Germans had intended to make short work of the slaughter, but this has resolved itself into an obstinate battle that has now been raging for five days. The Jewish population put up heroic resistance, attacking Hitler's bandits with hand-grenades, pistols and sub-machine-guns, forcing the Germans to retreat with heavy losses. This was their initial victory. Very soon the rising assumed the proportions of a full-scale war, forcing the Germans to throw into the engagement within the narrow confines of the ghetto regular military forces, artillery and tanks, and even aircraft. The Germans have now officially launched an offensive. Bitter battles are being waged over each house and each apartment. The ghetto walls, which were originally intended to assist the Germans in their bloody slaughter of the Jewish population, have turned the place into a veritable fortress, repeatedly assaulted for the fifth day now by the German monster. The ghetto is strewn with the corpses of German policemen and SS troopers, and Red Cross ambulances evacuate large numbers of wounded. This is not merely a military setback, but what is more a political defeat. The battle rages on. One cannot speak of the heroic efforts of the Jewish population without the deepest admiration and awe. Cut off from the world, tormented and massacred, driven to the lowest abyss of humiliation, the Jewish population has risen to make war on the mighty armed forces of the enemy."

And thus, the monumental struggle continued for 29 days! In fact, the resistance was finally broken only when the Germans decided to liquidate the ghetto with fire. In one of his final reports on the uprising, General Stroop writes: "In today's operation, several blocks of buildings were burned down. This is the only ultimate method of forcing this subhuman riff-raff to the surface". [7]

In the meantime both the ZOB and the ZZW fighters were nearing the moment when they would be out of both ammunition and manpower. Fighting side by side were the loyal friends of the ZZW—"Bystry's partisans. They too were heavily outnumbered. However they continued bravely to fight on and on, shoulder to shoulder with Appelbaum and his several comrades still able to resist.   In the meantime, "Bystry's" brother, group commander of the Polish resistance, was badly wounded. Appelbaum, too, received his second wound, this time in the lungs. He was in a bad state and should have been transferred to a place of safety. In fact, at one point, "Bystry" approached him and pleaded: "Maitek" (Appelbaum's pseudonym), why don't you come with us?" To which he answered: "I may be wounded but my mind is still working as it should. I know my people. I can't just leave them here. I have lived to see the most beautiful moment of my life, the moment to which I've devoted everything. I've seen my people fighting in battle. And this battle, in spite of everything, is going to end in our victory. I want to stay on in the fight to the end." He stayed behind and died the next day of exhaustion and hemorrhage. [8]

On May 17, 1943 the Warsaw Ghetto was no more. Some twenty five thousand Jews were still left alive, hiding out in the Aryan section of the city. Although desperate, hungry and weak, they searched for any opportunity to join Polish gentiles in their own uprising in the Warsaw area, which began on August 1, 1944. They looked to join the ranks of the insurgents only to find that they were not wanted. Both the N.S.Z. (the so-called National Armed Forces) as well as the A.K. extremists would not have any Jews fighting in their ranks and— more than that—they took the initiative in hunting them down and participating in their persecution and abuse. [9]

It should be recorded, however, that in spite of the continuing anti-Semitism of the Polish masses, there were many like "Bystry" and his comrades who helped the Jews and often protected them with their lives. Regretfully, these honorable citizens of Poland were in the minority. . . .

In view of the above listed facts, one is entitled to wonder how it was conceivable to suppress this super-human, heroic effort of Jabotinsky's followers from the records of history—a history hijacked by the monopoly of the Left-leaning journalists in the post-war Jewish world.

One of the reasons was the obvious, incurable hate by the Left which represented the attitude of "official" Zionism and dominated the Jewish media for the first 35 years of the existence of the State of Israel. However, there were also objective reasons that allowed for biased reporting on one hand, and curtailment of reports unacceptable to the Left leadership, on the other. These included the tragic fact that not a single commander of the ZZW survived. Inspired by the code of secrecy, which they no doubt adopted from the Israeli father-organization—the Irgun Zvai Leumi— the surviving rank and file was given no information whatsoever about the Organization's other members, its structure, battle plans and chain of command.

Also, the ostracism of the Jabotinsky Movement was easily abetted by the fact that these fighters of Zion did not engage in keeping diaries, notes or other historical records. Instead, they were busy composing and distributing leaflets and bulletins along with other cultural and educational activities. Hence the writing of history was completely monopolized by those who were bitterly hostile to the Jabotinsky Movement.

This was tragically reflected by the fact that the glorious efforts of Betarim, Revisionists and non-affiliated members of ZZW were hardly mentioned on the pages of "official" records of the Warsaw Ghetto uprising.

As we followed the evidence before us, it became quite clear that members of Jabotinsky's movement—*betarim*, Revisionists and the non-affiliated who joined the resistance—all strove towards a single aim: To form a mass resistance movement and direct it to strike a blow at the enemy, by turning the Warsaw ghetto into a bulwark of revolt and vengeance, that it may serve as a symbol of Jewish heroism for future generations. This was miraculously accomplished.

"The ZZW fighters did not engage in writing history," concludes Lazar in his eye-opening book on the Ghetto revolt—"Muranowska 7". "With rare foresight they realized that once their notion of mass resistance, which they conceived in the early days of the German occupation—materialized, the Warsaw ghetto rising would serve as a shining lesson for coming generations. Moreover, the fact that their contemporaries would not remember their names or record their heroic acts, would in no way detract from the greatness of the deed itself; on the contrary, the world would then know that every man, woman and child had shared equally in this supreme struggle for human dignity."

In the files of the Jewish Historical Institute of Warsaw, there is a letter written by a nameless Jew to his family in Palestine, from a bunker in Warsaw. The letter, which is dated 21 of July 1943, i.e. more than three months after the outbreak of the Warsaw ghetto rising, reads as follows: "On Passover we were ordered finally to leave the ghetto. But the boys and girls, our nameless soldiers, put up a proper resistance. The watchword was "For Life or Death! Let my soul die with the Philistines!" One thousand young men and women, armed with pistols, hand-grenades, machine-guns, bombs and the like, fought against the assassins and killed hundreds of SS troopers. Our young people were happy to leave this world in the knowledge that they had dispatched some of the murderers. I am the man that has seen all this. I asked the young people: "What are your names? Perhaps I may be granted redemption and your names will go down in history." But what they answered was 'It's not important. We wish to be the anonymous soldiers. All we want is the satisfaction of leaving this world in the knowledge that we have exacted some little revenge'. Yes, I must point out that the young people who volunteered belonged to every possible social grouping, ranging from the extreme right to the extreme left, but most of them were Revisionists." †

In concluding this chapter, at once the most tragic and most uplifting, it is difficult not to realize that in addition to the horrors-of the Nazi machinery of death, the isolations, the hostile populations and the bereavement of hope, the ghetto population was orphaned by the absence of any real leadership in its hour of darkness and desperation. Instead, they were led by spineless men of the Judenrat, who failed to realize the terrible danger and inadvertently aided the enemy. Worse still, was the ever present shadow of internal strife, adding painful and bitter tears to the rivers of blood shed by Zion and its faithful adherents.

It is in such conditions that the heroes of the Warsaw Ghetto rose in revolt.

And in spite of everything—theirs was the ultimate victory.

Notes

* Deportation Station
† The writer, whose name is unknown, requested that his letter, if found, be forwarded to his relatives in the Land of Israel. But who are they? The letter was discovered among a mass of material, in the Jewish Historical Institute, but no one knows how it got there or where it came from.

1. *Muranowska 7* by Chaim Lazar. Page 76. Published by Massada, Tel Aviv 1966
2. *Muranowska 7* by Chaim Lazar. Page 124
3. *Muranowska 7* by Chaim Lazar. Page 104
4. *The Struggle & Destruction of the Warsaw Ghetto* by Prof. Bernard Mark. Page 19
5. *Muranowska 7* by Chaim Lazar. Page 231
6. *Muranowska 7* by Chaim Lazar. Page 233
7. *Muranowska 7* by Chaim Lazar. Page 263
8. Commander Bystry's testimony as related by Chaim Lazar in *Muranowska 7*, Page 289
9. *Muranowska 7* by Chaim Lazar. Page 305

Chapter 6
Season of Treason

With the Warsaw Ghetto burning, the gas chambers consuming the remnants of European Jewry and our brethren in America passive and leaderless, the only hope that remained was with the half million Jews in mandated Eretz Israel.

In Palestine, Ben Gurion, although showing signs of disenchantment with Weizmann's courtship of Britain, was nevertheless leading the Haganah and the Jewish Agency into the self proclaimed policy of "havlaga" (restraint) vis-à-vis the violence being perpetrated by Palestinian Arabs.

The one group resisting these terrorists was the Hebrew underground called the Irgun Zvai Leumi, or ETZEL, for short. This was the militant arm of Jabotinsky followers composed of Revisionists, *Betarim* and even some disenchanted members of the Haganah. There were also some religious and unaffiliated youths who enthusiastically joined this Hebrew underground and shared its readiness to oppose by force both the Arab terror and the British occupation of their land.

At the time, the Irgun was led by a young *Betari*, handpicked by Jabotinsky for the task. His name was David Raziel.

David was a brave warrior, courageous and daring. He led the Irgun in counter attacks on Arab bands, protected the Jews assembling at the "Wailing Wall" in Jerusalem and participated in bringing "illegal" immigrants to the shores of Eretz Israel.

However, when the World War broke out, the Irgun encouraged the young men of the Yishuv to join the British armed forces in their struggle against the common enemy.

David Raziel was among the first to have volunteered his services. He was killed while performing a secret intelligence mission in Iraq, which was then occupied by the Nazis. After a period of Yishuv-wide mourning, the Irgun command was passed on to Raziel's second in command—Yaacov Meridor.

Orphaned by Raziel's death and deprived of an incentive for real action, many left the ranks of the Irgun to find solace in being involved in the war as His Majesty's conscripts. Nevertheless, Meridor faithfully held the organization together and devoted much time to training his men for future activities of the underground.

In the meantime, the fortunes of war began to smile on the Allies with decisive victories on the African front. The following year saw the Allied invasion of Sicily and the Italian mainland, followed by the collapse of the Mussolini regime.

Britain was no longer threatened by defeat. On the other hand, the remnants of European Jewry continued to be gassed in the death camps and Britain continued to bar Jews from reaching the safety of Palestinian shores.

By now, the Irgun leadership felt that time was ripe to renew the struggle for independence and to raise the banner of revolt against the British Colonial Administration.

It was at this time that Yaacov Meridor began to look for his own replacement. Somehow he felt that a more erudite politician and a more powerful leader was required for the tasks ahead. The question was: Who?

Although Meridor was a fine organizer, he lacked experience in the art of propaganda, which at this juncture was considered all-important. It was therefore agreed that the command should be turned over to an individual who had demonstrated skill in formulating and publicizing the political ideals which Irgun had meant to pursue. The choice fell on Menachem Begin.[1]

When the choice was finally made, it may have seemed to be the outcome of "pressure of the time." More intimately, however, it was undeniable that Begin's name was on everyone's mind the moment he entered Palestine as a private in Anderson's Polish army. In fact, he was the obvious choice.

Menachem Begin was Jabotinsky's personal choice to replace Aaron Propes as leader of Betar in Poland, when the latter was transferred to the United States. Although well known as organizer, orator and man of high integrity and wisdom, Begin did not have too much time to lead his *betarim* before Poland fell to the Germans and was subsequently divided between Hitler and Stalin.

Begin succeeded in escaping to Vilna together with his young wife Eliza and several comrades from Betar. From Vilna the group planned to cross into Rumania and from there to attempt boarding some vessel to the land of their dreams. However, while in Vilna, Begin was arrested by the Soviet Secret Police, separated from his wife and friends, led from interrogation to interrogation, convicted of treason against the Soviet Union and sentenced to hard labor in Russian jails and gulags. He was finally released after a year of confinement, under an agreement reached between Poland and Russia following Hitler's invasion of its former eastern "ally".

Thus it came about that Begin attempted to enlist into the Polish army while tracing his way out of the Siberian wilderness. During recruitment, a Polish officer assigned to interview him found Begin to be unacceptable due to his weak heart and weaker eyes. Undeterred, Begin scrawled a note to the officer's chief of staff imploring him to reconsider the decision of his subordinate. As a result, Begin was granted an audience during which he explained his fear of being re-arrested by the Soviets. The chief of staff relented but warned: "I'll keep an eye on you. Don't get it in your head to run off to Palestine once we head south!" Actually, he did not have to worry. The army moved to Persia, then westward and in May 1942, crossed into Transjordan and Palestine. [2]

Menachem Begin was discharged at the end of 1943 as a result of contacts made by Arie Ben Eliezer with the Polish ministry staff. Only now, he felt free to accede to his comrades' demand that he take over the command of the Irgun.

From the initial stages of his leadership, Begin was determined to outline the goals, plans and methods of his underground organization. In one of the very first of the myriads of his wall posters to the nation, Begin called for a revolt against the British Administration. This proclamation was posted on walls and kiosks throughout Palestine and addressed itself to "the Hebrew People in Zion." The proclamation, appearing on Feb. 1, 1944, said: "By ignoring the promises implicit in the Palestine Mandate and remaining unmoved while European Jewry was being slaughtered, the British had betrayed the Jewish People and there is no longer any moral basis for a British presence in Palestine." Begin then spelled out the Irgun demands of the British overlords: "Administrative authority in Palestine is to be transferred at once from the British Administration to a 'Hebrew Provisional Government'." As for the adjoining Arab nations, "the Hebrew Government would offer them a peace of honor and good neighborliness".

The proclamation also addressed itself to the internal policy of the future State: "Within the Jewish State to be created, the Government would undertake to ensure employment and 'social justice' for every citizen of the state and full equal rights for the Arab population. The Holy Places of the Christian and Moslem faiths would be guaranteed extraterritorial status".

And, by way of a postscript, the proclamation urged "all Jews in Palestine to help the Irgun in the struggle by acts of civil disobedience—refusing to pay taxes and organizing strikes and demonstrations". [3]

In the meantime Begin sent clear instructions to all officers and men of the underground. In these, he outlined Irgun's policy of confining all its activity of harassment to non-military targets of the British Administration, pending the successful conclusion of the war against Hitler. He also placed the Irgun men under strict orders to refrain from killing, except in order to save their own lives.

The latter policy of conduct was in clear contrast to the one endorsed by the more extreme splinter group, called "Fighters for the Freedom of Israel", but better know as the "Stern Group".*

After the split, leaders of the Irgun made several attempts at reunification. One of Irgun's leaders and a close associate of Begin was Eliahu Lankin—a betari from Harbin, China. In his book *"To Win the Promised Land"*, Lankin wrote: "The Irgun High Command sincerely desired unification with the Sternists since we believed this to be for the national good; but the many efforts at unification that were renewed from time to time, ultimately came to naught. It appeared that the Stern Group simply did not want unification. One of their reasons offered in favor of separate existence was their belief that as long as they existed, the Irgun would not dare end its war against the British. From our point of view, this argument had no validity and was childish as well." [4]

However the subject lost its urgency after the shocking event that was about to erupt. The explosion occurred on November 6, 1944, when two members of the Stern Group assassinated Lord Moyne, the British Minister of State for Middle Eastern Affairs. The assassination took place in Cairo and both participants were arrested, judged and finally executed by hanging.

Although the assassination had nothing whatsoever to do with the Irgun, Ben Gurion and the Haganah used this as a pretext to go after the Irgun, whom they considered to be their more serious adversary. Thus began the ignominious "Season"—the code name given to Haganah's campaign of betrayal of Irgun members to the British authorities.

Leaders of the Stern Group, in the meantime, pledged to cease their anti-British activities and consequently were left unmolested. More than this, they were even sheltered by the kibbutzim. Thus, although the Sternists provided the excuse, the "Season" was solely directed against the Irgun.

"Season" is a mild sounding concept. In reality it was the most vicious and brutal campaign of brother against brother since the days of Cain and Abel. At no time was the mood in Palestine darker. Pessimism spread like wild-fire as the specter of fratricide hovered near.

The main work of the "open season" was performed by the Haganah unit of volunteers, which had been trained especially for that purpose. Irgun men were shadowed, kidnapped and placed into improvised prisons at leftist kibbutzim. Worse, the British themselves were able to arrest hundreds of Irgunists with the help of lists turned over to them by the Haganah. [5]

Among those betrayed and arrested were the top leaders of the underground, such as Yaacov Meridor, Eliahu Lankin and Arie Ben Eliezer—all members of the Irgun High Command.

Many years after the War of Independence, some leaders of the Left attempted to deny involvement in this shameful episode of betrayal and treason. They attempted to blame it on some "hot heads" among their youth, and claimed that the "Season" was at no time the official policy of either Ben Gurion or the Haganah.

This has been decisively proven to be false as witnessed by several independent accounts.

On November 20, 1944 Ben Gurion called on Jews to "deny all succor to the terrorists and help hand them over to the British". [6] In December of the same year Dr. Chaim Weizmann cabled Winston Churchill, then Prime Minister of Great Britain. The cable read, in part: "I fully realize the gravity of the situation. Our cooperation with the authorities in stamping out terrorism is proceeding satisfactorily. Five hundred names of suspects have already been supplied to the police as a result of whom over two hundred and fifty have been arrested. Effective cooperation has been tendered, also in other forms. It is confidentially believed that severe blows have been already dealt to them and there is every determination to persevere with the campaign until decisive results are achieved. We can only do our best". [7]

There is not a shred of evidence to be found which would contradict the facts, proving enthusiastic involvement of Weizmann, Ben Gurion and the Haganah in this dark chapter of Jewish history.

Not only were Jews taught to deny their soldiers of the underground shelter, jobs and moral support, they were also urged to betray them to the enemy of the Jewish cause and to personally participate in inflicting physical torture on their brothers.

One of the victims of such brutality was Eliahu Ravid, Lankin's comrade in Tel-Aviv. A detachment of Palmach men descended on Eliahu and led him on foot to Pinsker Street, near the Mugrabi Theatre. A pick-up truck awaited them there. After Ravid climbed in, he was blind-folded and his hands were tied. Till today he does not know where he was taken. That night, Ravid was brought to a cave. "In the cave stood an iron bed-stead and a lantern. Ravid was chained to the bed and remained chained during the four months of his captivity. During the interrogations that followed his arrest, Ravid would hear screams of pain and moaning from adjacent rooms." [8]

At the same time the Haganah succeeded in capturing Eli Tavin, head of Irgun's intelligence department. Eli was kidnapped and chained to a bed for six months at Kibbutz Ein Harod. "He had been blindfolded, subjected to a mock execution, beaten, and chained to a steel cot in a darkened store-room for weeks on end". [9]

Another victim of sadism of the Jewish socialists was Mordechai Raanan who would later become the commander of Irgun's forces fighting in Jerusalem. During the "Season" he too was captured by the Haganah, at a bus stop. "We want to know who your commanders are, where you keep your weapons and who finances you." he was asked by the Haganah officer. "Do you think I'm going to tell you that?" Raanan replied. The following day he found himself in a cave, chained to an iron-slotted bed by wrists and ankles, while drops of rainwater dripped maddeningly on his face. When, after six days and nights he still refused to talk, they finally let him go—a numbed, hungry animal, covered with filth and barely able to walk. [10]

In his brief comments, Eliahu Lankin, himself a victim of these treacherous acts (he was one of the first of the Irgun High Command to be betrayed, arrested and deported to Eritrea) writes in his book *"To Win the Promised Land"*: "From all this evidence—particularly when examined in the light of events that followed—it is clear beyond any doubt that not only did the "Season" constitute official policy, but the Haganah also intended thereby to destroy the Irgun. The "Season" was directed by Jews against Jews and was simply a maneuver devised to seize power. To that end the perpetrators did not hesitate to kidnap and torture their brethren, cooperate with the British CID and betray Jewish fighters to the British Authorities." [11]

By now resentment reached a boiling point within rank and file of the

Hebrew underground. The mildest and the calmest of the Irgun officers began to demand an appropriate reaction. But Begin stood fast.

Angry, frustrated and hurt, he continued to maintain his principle of "Fratricide?—Never!" And it was in keeping to this faith that he issued a statement severely berating Ben Gurion and his Haganah brass:

> "You rampage, Cain, in the Streets of Jerusalem, in Tel-Aviv, in the towns and villages. You have used your might. But you did not use it when millions of our brothers perished as they turned their eyes to Zion."
>
> "You chose an ally, Cain. To them, you turned over your brothers—into hands stained with the blood of millions thrown back from the gates of the homeland into the ovens of Maidanek..."
>
> "Cars chase cars. Telephones ring. Signals are given and detectives appear. Tommy guns are raised. 'Halt!'—the foreign rulers command. 'Out of the cars', the enslavers order. 'Which one?' the detectives—your allies—ask. And you, Cain, walk over, raise your hand, and point: 'That's him. Take him!'"
>
> "Your mouth brims with socialist rhetoric, Cain, but you are an exploiter. You incite, inform, betray, abduct, and hand men over, Cain."
>
> "And we, the soldiers of Zion, are commanded not to repay you. Though our blood boils, it is blood that is totally dedicated to the nation and the homeland. Our eyes are directed, even today—especially today!—toward love of our brothers, toward the redemption of our nation."[12]

The self discipline which rallied the entire rank and file of the Irgunists to Begin's decision against retaliation, earned the Irgun, and Begin, the respect of friends and opponents alike. Even those who did not always agree with Irgun's methods of operation began to suspect that the Labor Zionists had gone way overboard in proclaiming an "open season" on the "dissidents." The "men on the street" began to suspect that the "hunters" of the Left might well have been motivated by partisan considerations, more specifically, to keep non-Laborites from gaining influence, power and respect in the future Jewish State.

Even the Chief Rabbinate, which occasionally voiced its disapproval of Irgun's operations for fear of British retaliation, was now openly condemning Haganah's kidnappings and other anti-Irgun excesses.

As the winter of 1944 was gradually yielding to the spring of 1945, the Jewish Agency itself began to realize that the "Season" has boomeranged and the average opinion in the Ishuv was becoming increasingly critical of the Haganah and the Labor leadership. The only thing the "Season" accomplished was to earn growing sympathy for the Irgun, while casting a shadow of suspicion over the Agency's motives.

Thus, by May 1945, as the war in Europe came to an end, the "open season"—the season of treason—also came to its inglorious close.

Notes

* The Stern Group was a splinter of the Irgun, commanded by Avraham Stern. It promoted war against the British—war with no restrictions—even as the British were engaged in fighting the Germans. Stern, the leader, was murdered by the British CID in cold blood, but the Stern Group continued its separate existence under the command of Friedman-Yellin Mor, until Statehood was achieved.

1. *Menachem Begin* by Hirschberg and Beckman. New York, Page 68; Published by Shangold Publishers
2. *To Win or to Die* by Ned Temko. William Morrow Publishers. NY. Page 65
3. *Menachem Begin* by Hirschler and Eckman. Shangold Publishers. NY. Pages 72-73
4. *To Win the Promised Land* by Lankin. Pages 77-78
5. *Menachem Begin* by Hirschier and Eckman. Page 98
6. *Menachem Begin* by Hirschier and Eckman. Page 96
7. *To Win the Promised Land* by Lankin, Pages 107
8. *To Win the Promised Land* by Lankin. Pages 104-105
9. *To Win Or To Die* by Ned Temko, Published by W. Morrow. New York, Page 86
10. *Genesis 1948* by Dan Kurzman. World Publishing Co. New York. Page 544
11. *To Win the Promised Land* by Lankin. Page 107
12. *To Win or To Die* by Ted Temko. Page 84

Chapter 7
A Tragic Road to Victory

In spite of the miserable failure of the "season" and the wide public acclaim for Begin and the Jewish underground which resisted fratricide, it took more than remorse to convince Ben Gurion to abandon his vendetta against the followers of Zeev Jabotinsky. In fact, it took a powerful slap on the face, delivered by the Mandate Authority on June 29, 1946, when the British made a dawn swoop on the Jewish Agency, arresting hundreds, including the top leadership of the Palestinian Jewry.

As a result, Ben Gurion ordered the Haganah to extend a hand in peace and cooperation to both the Irgun and the Stern Group. Immediately, negotiations began with representatives of each organization in order to formalize targets, methods and schedules of future military action in Palestine.

The concept of joint planning and execution was eagerly accepted by both the Irgun and the Stern Group's leadership. In fact they both expressed readiness to fight under Ben Gurion's command, as long as the latter was prepared to commit himself to the revolt against the British Authority.

Ben Gurion, though unwilling to go the "full distance" was ready to form an organization named "Tnuat Hameri" (The United Resistance Movement) incorporating the Haganah, the Irgun and the Stern Group. Although each one of the three could operate separately, all plans and executions were to be approved and scheduled in advance by the "Joint Command".

Coming in the midst of a brutal struggle for Zion's very existence, this was regarded as the "finest hour of Zionism"—a united Hebrew front aimed at liberating Eretz Israel!

It was during these days and nights of united combat, that the Irgun introduced its previously conceived plan to blow up the King David Hotel in Jerusalem—a hotel turned into the center of British intelligence and administration. The joint command approved the concept and the plan, leaving the date of execution indeterminate.

In the meantime in separate actions British police headquarters were attacked, trains sabotaged, arms confiscated, bridges blown up and illegal immigrants successfully smuggled.

Chapter 7

The most outstanding of these operations was the Irgun's assault on the central airfield at Kastina. The soldiers of the Irgun came well prepared. They even brought along with them little ladders on which they climbed atop the great steel bodies of the planes. In went the explosives and within moments—the heavy four-engine Halifax bombers were reduced to useless steel.

The joy of the Jewish people was even greater than the consternation of the British Authorities. In summarizing his brief account of this attack in his book *"The Revolt"*, Menachem Begin writes: "At first we of the Irgun were silent. The Haganah had asked us not to publish any statement that would identify the attacking organizations. We agreed. The glorification of our arms was far less important than the fact that a united people were now fighting the oppressor. But the Haganah changed its mind and in an urgent note asked us to accept responsibility for destroying the British planes. So be it. We readily complied. The public was astounded. In the streets of the towns you could see long queues reading every word of our communiqué. People exclaimed in wonderment: 'So the dissidents are capable of such things!' They did not trouble to hide their enthusiasm even from the British authorities. In a Tel Aviv cafe a British officer asked for his check. The proprietor replied: 'You don't owe us anything. You paid us yesterday—with thirty planes.' [1]

Those days of the joint resistance were happy days indeed. They were days of dangerous actions, enormous sacrifices and painful losses. But they were also days of glory, achievement and unity. Menachem Begin recalled that "These were the best days of my life".

It was at this time that Britain was especially active in its attempt to turn back shiploads of Jewish refugees from death camps in Europe, sailing towards the shores of the "Promised Land". The Irgun command believed that it was time to retaliate with their "'King David Hotel" plan. After several pleas for postponement, the Resistance Movement accepted the plan and agreed on the date of its execution.

However, on July 19, Moshe Sneh of the Haganah, representing Ben Gurion himself, sent a note to Begin requesting an additional postponement of the attack for a few days. The Irgun acceded to the request, accepting a new date of July 22 as the final day for action.

It was therefore on July 22 that the Irgun commandos placed two milk cans in the basement of the King David Hotel.

At the prescribed hour, the Irgun telephonist contacted the receptionist at the hotel to warn: "Evacuate the whole building! Bombs have been placed in the hotel and it must be evacuated immediately!" A similar message was telephoned to the Jerusalem English language newspaper, the Palestine Post. A third warning was phoned in to the French Consulate located across from the hotel, advising them to open the windows in the building to prevent possible injuries from the blast.

At 12:37 the whole town seemed to shudder. "The force of the explosion was even greater than expected. The milk cans reached the whole height of the building from basement to roof and the entire wing of the hotel was cut off as with a knife." [2]

Tragically, the warnings of the Irgun were ignored. As Begin subsequently learned, the warning was ridiculed by a British high official, who exclaimed: "We are not here to take orders from the Jews. We give them orders". [3]

On request of the Haganah, the Irgun did not publish any statements identifying itself as the attacking body on the day of the operation. But there seemed to be no end to confusion within the Haganah leadership itself. One officer at first advised the Jewish Press not on any account, to denounce the operation, hinting broadly that the Haganah had had prior knowledge of the attack. Later in the day, when it became known that there had been many casualties, he advised the press to make no comment at all, positive or negative. His third directive instructed the newspapers to denounce the "dissidents" (meaning the Irgun and the Stern Group) unreservedly.[4]

Why was the King David Hotel an important target? Simply put—it was because of its southern wing, which housed the central institutions of the British regime: Military G.H.Q., the Secretariat and the civil Government.

This bald assault caused the British a major embarrassment and loss of prestige throughout the world. To offset their defeat at the hands of the Hebrew underground, they attempted to portray the assailants as blood thirsty murderers seeking innocent victims and defenseless civilians for their brutal crimes. The world knew different. What did hurt the cause of Zion however, was the about face of the Haganah and the Left leaders' revival of denunciations and abuse.

Either for fear of renewed arrests and retaliation by the British or prompted by their expectations of a world wide condemnation of the Irgun, the Left quickly abandoned its previous pledge of cooperation and renewed, with enhanced force, the sharp and vicious condemnations of the Jewish underground.

The joint resistance movement vanished into thin air. Indeed the days of smiles and happiness were short and few, while the days of tears and sorrow were long and many.

Yet, at a later date, the British themselves admitted that the blowing up of the King David Hotel along with the hanging of their sergeants and the storming of the Acco prison-fortress* were all acts of the Irgun that drove the British out of Palestine. [5]

By now, the actions of the Irgun caused frustration and anger within the British Parliament. Statesmen of record, including the head of the opposition, Sir Winston Churchill, began demanding surrender of the Mandate to the United Nations. .The massive assault on British military power and political prestige became too heavy a burden to bear. However, the British Labor Government was in no mood to "surrender to the terrorists". They planned to regain prestige and position themselves for a continued dominating role on the Middle Eastern political stage.

Thus, they built gallows and instituted military trials, country-wide curfews and severe whippings of "terrorist hooligans", who were too young to be executed. But, in spite of renewed denunciations by the Jewish Authority and the Haganah, the Irgun succeeded in retaliating for whippings with whippings and hangings with hangings.

Finally, the mighty British Empire decided to surrender its Mandate and to accept the UN partition plan to divide the territory of Palestine (minus Transjordan) into Jewish and Arab States.

Although Jabotinsky's followers, led by Begin and the Irgun, denounced and ridiculed the partition of Eretz Israel, they accepted Ben Gurion's decision to create a Jewish state on land liberated with Jewish arms and to await an opportune time to eventually return to the historic borders of Eretz Israel.

The Arabs, on the other hand, rejected the partition completely.

In the meantime, no one was naive enough to wait for the announced date of British withdrawal from Palestine—May 14, 1947. The Arabs, with British help, were securing weapons and bases, entrenching themselves in British-held police stations, while Ben Gurion agreed to join forces again with the Irgun and the Stern Group in an attempt to secure as much territory as possible from the "allocated" parts of the partition and as much adjacent land of the mandated territory, which was meant to be the "Jewish National Home", as possible.

The three organizations—Haganah, Irgun and Stern—were pretty much left on their own. However, Ben Gurion's overall command of the operations was accepted and respected, once again.

One of the urgent military problems was created by the Arab assault on the Tel Aviv-Jerusalem highway, thus depriving Jerusalem of supplies, rearmament and regularity of contact with the rest of the country.

The "bone in the throat" was an Arab village—Dir Yassin located off the highway on the slopes leading to the city of David. As part of the overall plan to liberate Jerusalem, the Irgun commander in the area, Mordechai Raanan, prepared an assault on Dir Yassin, with the help of forces from the Stern Group, commanded by Yehoshua Zetler.

Although it was soon to be disputed, the action was approved by Haganah's regional commander—Shaltiel, who dispatched a letter to Raanan on the eve of battle. The letter read, in part: "I learnt that you plan to attack Dir Yassin. I wish to point out that the capture of Dir Yassin and holding it is one stage in our general plan. I have no objection to your carrying out the operation provided you are able to hold the village." [6]

The battle for Dir Yassin began with loudspeakers announcing the surrounding of the village and demanding immediate surrender. In response, fire erupted from every hut. As a result, the loudspeakers blared out a final demand: "Evacuate women and children—they can take shelter on the slope of the hill". However, many did not leave. As a result, Begin recalls: "The fire of the enemy was murderous—to which the number of our casualties bare eloquent testimony. Our men were compelled to fight for every house, to overcome the enemy they used large numbers of hand grenades. The civilians who stayed behind suffered inevitable casualties." [7]

When the battle was won, more than 200 Arabs of the village were dead. Among them were women and children. Irgun and the Stern Group suffered heavy losses as well. Some accounts claim 40 dead and wounded Irgunists and Sternists. Such was the price paid for the Dir Yassin victory. . . .

Of course the Arab press publicized Dir Yassin as a "slaughter of innocents". This was to be expected and had come as no surprise. In fact, each time Arab aggression was successfully repelled, they screamed foul and invented stories of horrors and atrocities.

What was totally uncalled for and painfully destructive was the campaign of denunciation and abuse waged, once again, by Ben Gurion and the Left-controlled press in Palestine. It was based on such exaggerated reports of "criminal abuse" and "wanton murder" that the world drew its picture of the Dir Yassin operation. Not only were these reports viciously slanted and often "doctored," they were primarily aimed to disqualify the Irgun from any serious considerations for leadership in the forthcoming independent Jewish State. In the meantime, what it did achieve was to besmirch the honor and the pure character of Jewish fighters for liberty and statehood.

All explanations and factual reports of the battle for Dir Yassin were drowned in the avalanche of insults, abuse and fabrications, which contaminated both the local and the international media. As a result, the successful and costly assault on Dir Yassin became a dirty word. And it remains so till today.

In spite of this breach of cooperation by the Haganah and the Jewish Agency, the Irgun continued to concentrate on securing the future borders of the Jewish State. Their next target was to liberate Jaffa on the outskirts of Tel Aviv.

Jaffa was an ancient seaport protected by the British on one hand and the British trained Jordanian Legion, on the other.

It was from Jaffa that sporadic gunfire was indiscriminately directed towards the streets and the buildings of Tel Aviv.

The UN partition allocated Jaffa to the future "Arab Palestinian State." Of course, if it would have remained in Arab hands after the British departure, foreign armies from Syria, Egypt and Iraq would have been invited to supplement the Arab Legion from Jordan, already there. This would have placed Tel Aviv in mortal danger.

On the night of April 25, 1948, with the British still in the country, the Irgun battle units assembled at Ramat Gan, a city of gardens neighboring Tel Aviv. For the first time ever, their mystic commander in chief, Menachem Begin, and the chief of operations—Giddy Palgin, appeared before the troops and explained their historic mission: Occupation of Jaffa—Liberation of Tel Aviv!

The first night and day of battle yielded no results. The enemy fought hard and the Irgun suffered heavy casualties. By the second day there were serious thoughts of abandoning the assault to spare the attackers from further casualties.

With the dawn came the newspapers reporting "abortive" attack on Jaffa. One paper branded the attack "barren." Another accused the Irgun of "exhibitionism". All the terms were similar and it was quite obvious that the tune of denunciations and ridicule was "orchestrated" and "inspired" from one source.

Soon the source exposed itself. The Haganah Command issued a communiqué couched in 'similar terms announcing Irgun's failure in their attack on Jaffa and suggesting that "after all the Irgun was less concerned with capturing the streets of Jaffa than the votes of Tel Aviv."†

Here it was for all to see: Jewish boys fighting and dying to relieve their "Jewish city of Tel Aviv" from Arab bullets, while "official" leaders of the Yishuv—the leftists of the Haganah and the leadership of Mapai—sitting and gloating that the Irgun has failed.

In "The Revolt", Begin asked: "Could there be a more revolting attitude than this? Was this not yet another example of the shameful self-hatred that has plagued us Jews ever since we were exiled from our country nearly two thousand years ago?" [8]

While these vulgar attacks of the press and Zionist officialdom were taking place, Giddy, the Irgun commander of the assault forces, launched a new attack on Jaffa from the ruins of buildings destroyed the previous night. This time the Irgun men succeeded to break through the defenses and reached the area at the northern approaches of the city of Jaffa. Thus the enemy lines were cut in two. Now, Arab positions began to fall one after the other. As a result, the Arab civilians of Jaffa and a variety of Arab fighters suddenly began to leave the town in panic.

However, at this point the British reneged on their agreement not to interfere and began to bombard the attacking Irgun forces. The battle raged for several hours but the British failed to dislodge the Jewish attackers from their forward positions.

During the combat, the Irgun command warned the British to withdraw to their barracks. Otherwise, the Irgun threatened that the agreed upon "peaceful withdrawal of British forces from Palestine," will be seriously jeopardized. Finally, an agreement was reached: The Irgun forces would not enter the city itself but continue to hold positions bordering with Tel Aviv.

However, early in May, some ten days before the British withdrawal from Palestine, the fate of Jaffa was sealed. The Arab "Emergency Committee" composed of Arab civilians of Jaffa signed the surrender of the town. It was received by the Haganah's Tel Aviv Regional Commander. As a result, the town was occupied jointly by the Haganah and the Irgun units.

Another great victory of Hebrew arms, tarnished by internal friction, dissent and abuse.

On Friday, May 14, 1948, Ben Gurion rose to the podium in the old exhibition gallery of the museum on the sea shore of Tel Aviv and announced to the world: "By virtue of our national and intrinsic right and on the strength of the resolution of the United Nations General Assembly, we hereby declare the establishment of a Jewish State in Palestine, which will be known as the State of Israel."

Immediately following this declaration, applauded by every Jewish citizen of Israel and most Jews and gentiles throughout the world, Ben Gurion announced his Provisional Government. In it he included almost every political party in the country. However, he proudly proclaimed that "'Herut' and the pro-Soviet communist party were the only two groups he would never invite into his government." [9]

"Herut", of course, was the political party formed by Begin and his colleagues of the Irgun High Command. Having declared acceptance of Ben Gurion as Prime Minister and his Government as the Government of Israel, Begin announced the disbandment of the Irgun within the borders controlled by the Jewish Government. At the same time the Irgun would continue its independent activity, along with the Palmach and the Stern Group, in the "old city" of Jerusalem.

The fact that he was ignored, side-stepped and insulted did not deter Begin from calling the People of Israel to remain loyal to the Provisional Government and join it in the struggle for independence and liberty. In his first public radio address to the nation, he declared:

> "The Irgun Z'vai Leumi is now leaving the underground within the borders of the independent Hebrew state. We went down underground—or better, we went up underground—under a foreign regime of oppression, to beat it and to liquidate it. And we beat it. We beat it good and destroyed it forever. Now we have Hebrew rule, (even if) for the time being it is only in part of our homeland, in this part of our homeland . . . there is no (longer any) need for a Hebrew underground. In the State of Israel, we shall be soldiers and builders. We shall abide by its laws, for they are our laws. We shall respect its government, for it is our government." [10]

After he finished his broadcast, Begin and his comrades left the Irgun radio station and proceeded to an important midnight meeting with Israel Galili and two other representatives of the Haganah. The meeting was called at Begin's request to discuss certain developments that were taking place at a seaport in southern France. As it turned out, these events would lead to what Begin attempted so diligently and consistently to avoid—Jews killing Jews.

In the meantime, Jews everywhere were celebrating the second deliverance: Jewish State was born anew! It came at a heavy price of blood and tears. And more of both were yet to be shed.

Notes

* A brilliantly planned attack of the Acco jail by the forces of the Irgun, freed dozens of imprisoned members of the underground and was considered to be "the greatest jail break in history".

† During the years prior to the establishment of the Jewish State, the leaders of the Mapai Party were the dominant political group in Palestine. They regarded the Irgun as a dangerous threat to their political influence. Hence every achievement of the Jabotinsky

followers was regarded as a threat to their dominance.
1. *The Revolt* by Menachem Begin, Nash Publishing, NY. 1978, Pages 264-265
2. *The Revolt* by Begin. Pages 294-295
3. *The Revolt* by Begin. Page 296
4. *The Revolt* by Begin. Page 298
5. *The Revolt* by Begin. Page 380
6. *The Revolt* by Begin. Page 225
7. *The Revolt* by Begin. Page 226
8. *The Revolt* by Begin. Page 464
9. *To Win or Die* by Ned Temko. Page 133
10. *Menachem Begin* by Hirschier and Eckman. Page 155

Chapter 8
Altalena

Even among Jabotinsky's most fervent followers only a few knew that he chose his pen name "Altalena" by mistake.

While switching his contributions of regular feuilletons* from Odessky Listok to Odesskiya Novosti in 1898, Jabotinsky decided to chose a pseudonym in the belief that "Altalena," in Italian, stands for "elevator". It turned out that the real meaning of "Altalena" is "swing." After discovering his error, Jabotinsky wrote to his new editor, Heifetz, explaining that he "felt, as yet, by no means stable or constant, but rather rocking and balancing—so that the pen name "swing" fitted him all right". [1] And he never bothered to change it.

Of course, in years that followed, while writing from Italy, Jabotinsky took time to master the Italian language to such a degree that soon he was able to converse in 12 accents, covering all existing dialects—which was a fete rarely followed by too many Italians themselves. Jabotinsky's biographer, associate and friend, Dr. Yoseph Borisovich Schechtman, recalls: "He became Italianized to an amazing degree; he frequented Italian circles only and learned to speak Italian without a trace of an accent; however, he later would joke that the people of the South regarded him a Northerner and vice versa, and that he never met anyone who took him for an Italian from his own province." [2]

The mistake never bothered Jabotinsky. For years that followed, "Altalena" became better known for the man beneath the pseudonym rather than for the meaning behind Jabotinsky's pen name with which he signed so many of his memorable feuilletons.

Almost fifty years to the day Jabotinsky "mistakenly" adopted "Altalena" as his nom de plume, his followers used the "swing" with which to honor their friend, mentor and leader.

****

As the British were packing their bags to leave Palestine, the Yishuv was faced with the danger of annihilation, as it stood surrounded by Arab armies from five adjacent states, as well as armed gangs organized by the Mufti of

Jerusalem.

The Haganah, following the lead of the Vaad Leumi, headed by Ben Gurion and his Mapai party, placed its trust in the United Nations' ability and desire to preserve peace and enforce its partition plan on all citizens of Palestine.

The Irgun Command, on the other hand, appealed continuously for joint action in procuring the necessary arms and bringing in trained volunteers from Jewish centers around the globe. As in previous instances, these appeals fell on deaf ears.

Thus, the Irgun was left to act on its own. The major problem was money. The coffers of the underground organization were always empty. The only Irgun affiliated body with some means at their disposal, was Bergson's group in the USA.

Since the Group was involved with bringing in "illegal" immigrants to Palestine, it gradually became familiar with the shipping industry and knew the market for available LST vessels, discarded after the Second World War.

Bergson's Hebrew Committee appointed Abrasha Stavsky (of Arlozoroff case fame) to be in charge of organizing a shipping company which would procure an appropriate vessel for carrying men and weapons from Europe to Palestine.

Thus it came about on a summer day in 1947 that a vessel was bought, with the funds of the Hebrew Committee, which was designed to load tanks and men during amphibious invasions. It was an LST of 4,500 tons. diesel-powered. about 100 feet wide and 300 feet long. The ship was capable of traveling long distances at fairly high speeds. Hundreds of similar ships were available at bargain prices, for they were left-over from Allies' North African and Normandy invasions. [3]

It was obvious to all concerned that this ship should be named after Zeev Jabotinsky. "However," recalls Eliahu Lankin, "to name the ship openly 'The Zeev Jabotinsky' was too dangerous, as it would attract the attention of our enemies. We knew that British Intelligence was active in sabotage of ships acquired for illegal immigration to Eretz Israel. We did not want to see any more Jews diverted to Cyprus where they would languish, unable to aid the cause that was so dear to their hearts. We needed to find a name that would be understood by the friends of Zion while remaining obscure to the rest of the world. I do not know who first conceived the idea of naming the ship 'Altalena', which was Jabotinsky's pen name at the start of his journalistic career in the early 1900's. However, it was this name that became the banner for our project to carry trained soldiers and badly needed weapons to the fighters in Eretz Israel. It became a symbol of idealism and dedication to our cause." [4]

The difference between *Altalena* and other boats procured for the purpose of ferrying new immigrants was in the concept of bringing both weapons and trained soldiers to the shores of Eretz Israel. Since "official" Zionism refused to participate in the project, it was up to the Irgun to purchase the boat. load it with weapons, train the soldiers for combat and equip the vessel with a professional crew. With Irgun's limited financial resources, this was almost an impossible task.

Nevertheless, Menachem Begin declared the *Altalena* project to be the central activity for all branches of the Jabotinsky Movement. Funds had to be accumulated from wherever possible. Weapons had to be bought and assembled at a "friendly port" somewhere in Europe. It was indeed a gigantic task, pregnant with difficulties and dangers.

The financial campaign to acquire funds for the *Altalena* project was called "Keren ha Barzel" (the Iron Fund) and it was conducted in every corner of the world including even the smallest Jewish Community. Per capita, the biggest success came from China, where a Jewish community of some fifteen thousand collected more than US $100,000— within one month of campaigning.

In the meantime, the Irgun representatives in Europe successfully contacted officials of the French government and received their blessing to procure a large quantity of arms, most of which would be given "gratis". Evidently, foreign minister George Bidault, like other French leaders of those days, was still bitter towards Britain for forcing the French out of Syria and Lebanon and was only too anxious to support a cause that would reduce British power in the Middle East.[5]

While Irgun men in Europe were being trained for combat and the French army was shipping the promised weapons to a central warehouse in Miramar, near Marseilles, Menachem Begin with Landau at his side, met with Ben Gurion's representatives—Igal Yadin and Israel Galili—to arrange details of incorporating the disbanded Irgun forces into the army of Israel.

It was finally agreed that whereas the Irgun would continue to operate independently in areas of Eretz Israel which will remain outside of control by the Government of Israel, the Irgun would cease to function within the borders of the partitioned Jewish State and its forces will be integrated into the army in complete battalions with their own officers. Likewise Begin informed the representatives of the Haganah that *Altalena* is being loaded in France, with men and weapons and was scheduled to reach Tel Aviv in the latter part of May. Again, the Haganah was invited to include their recruits from Europe to join the Irgun volunteers aboard the *Altalena*. The Haganah—declined.

Back in France, there were unforeseen delays in the arrangements, as a result of which *Altalena* was not ready to begin its voyage until June 11. By midnight June 9, with the aid of French soldiers and stevedores, the loading of weapons—all in wooden crates—was successfully completed: 5,000 rifles, 300 Bren guns, 150 Spandaus, 5 caterpillar-track armored cars, 4 million rounds of ammunition, several thousand air-combat bombs and other equipment.[6] On the following day, *Altalena's* captain Monroe Fein—an American Jew and an admirer of Jabotinsky and the Irgun, who volunteered as *Altalena's* captain, gave orders to lift anchor. Destination: Tel Aviv!

Captained by Fein, the ship's commander was Eliahu Lankin who was assisted by Abrasha Stavsky, Joe Cohen, Shmuel Merlin and Natan German (who was in charge of the arsenal). There were 940 recruits on board with enough crated weapons to equip ten battalions. The medical facilities and all necessary medical equipment were handled by another volunteer—Dr. Lazarev. *Altalena* was finally on its way.

The first word Begin received that the boat had sailed was not from the *Altalena* (which developed a malfunction of its radio transmitter from the first hour after leaving the shores of France) but rather from a BBC report late in the evening of June 11. That report followed the announcement that the Arab-Israeli truce began and that its terms included agreement by both sides not to import additional troops or weapons into the fighting zone while the truce lasted. [7]

An urgent meeting was arranged between Begin, Landau and Meridor representing the Irgun and Galili, Hacohen, Shkolnik** and Vaze representing the Haganah. Begin was aware of the fact that *Altalena's* arrival may cause a problem for the Government. He did not want to take the responsibility for breaking the truce. "You gentlemen are the representatives of the Government" he said. "It is you, not I, who must decide whether, under the present circumstances, the boat should be permitted to come here, or whether she should be diverted."[8]

Galili asked for some time "to figure things out" and after reporting to Ben Gurion, came back the next day to announce the Government's decision: *Altalena* was to proceed to Israel as quickly as possible and, in the meantime, Ben Gurion instructed Galili and his staff "to work out the details of the landing of the ship, the unloading of its cargo and the distribution of the weapons". [9]

As the news of this meeting reached Paris, Ben Eliezer joyfully exclaimed to Shmuel Katz: "There are no more internal problems. The *Altalena* can now sail. Full speed ahead!" †

In Tel Aviv Begin believed that everything has now been settled in principal. There was just a matter of arms distribution that had to be discussed. But, in view of Galili's cooperative handling of the previous negotiations, Begin believed that these details too, would be agreed upon with no problems. This however, was a mistake.

In Begin's mind 20% of the weapons would be turned over to the Irgun units still fighting independently in Jerusalem, while 80% would be distributed to the Irgun men on all fronts, who have now joined the Israeli army, but who, Begin believed, were being discriminated against by former Haganah officers when it came to the distribution of weapons.

When Begin presented this concept to Galili, the latter raised no objections that 20% of the weapons should go to the Irgun contingent in Jerusalem but refused to entertain the notion that the other 80% should go to the Irgunists in the Israeli army. In reply, Begin asked: "Wouldn't you agree that our boys should come into the army at least fully armed and equipped? You yourself" he continued, "demanded that in view of the gravity of the situation all arms and equipment in the possession of the Irgun should be issued to the Irgun boys who were going into the army. What has changed? Our boys are already in the army or will be within a matter of days. It will only mean that they will be mobilized with full equipment which we would have given them, in any case. What is wrong with that? Why can't you agree?" [10]

The discussion continued the next day. In the meantime, after an internal review of the matter, the Irgun decided to drop their demand for the 80% of the arms. The Irgun will be satisfied as long as 20% would be sent to its contingent, isolated in Jerusalem. To this Galili replied that it can be worked out and "20% will go to Jerusalem". Although he did not repeat the previous understanding verbatim, Begin took it for granted that Galili meant the Irgun units in Jerusalem.

As it turned out, Galili and Ben Gurion had already decided between themselves that 20% should not go to the Irgun but to the Haganah detachment which was also holding out in Jerusalem.... [11]

Begin's next meeting was with Pinhas Vaze from the Ministry of Defense, to determine the place for landing of the *Altalena*. According to Vaze, the boat should not dock in Tel Aviv, where it would obviously attract attention. Instead, he proposed landing the *Altalena* at Kfar Vitkin, to the north of Tel Aviv, just south of Natanya. This was accepted with no further discussion.

By now *Altalena* was approaching the coast line of Israel. When Lankin heard the news from Begin (on *Altalena's* repaired radio) he could hardly believe his ears. Excited and happy, he explained to Captain Fein, that Kfar Vitkin was a stronghold of Labor Zionists and if the Government chose Kfar Vitkin as the landing site for *Altalena*, it must mean that the Irgun is assured of full cooperation in landing and unloading of the boat.

It must be carefully noted that there was no attempt by the Irgun to bring the *Altalena* in during the truce period. The decision whether it should or should not attempt landing during the truce was made by the Government of Israel. This is an indisputable fact, well documented and easily proven.

On the day of *Altalena's* arrival, during the final meeting between Begin and Galili, neither one even touched upon the subject of truce and how to proceed with the ship's landing—in spite of it. The subject occupying their attention was the distribution of arms. It was at this meeting, held in the garden city of Ramat Gan that Galili struck the first note of alarm for Begin. Suddenly, he conveyed a blunt warning directly from Ben Gurion, instructing Begin and his associates to comply with "all Government's terms relevant to the landing and unloading of the *Altalena*, or else bear full responsibility for the consequences, and the responsibility will be heavy indeed". [12]

In parting, Galili added: "Unless Begin will change his mind; we will wash our hands of unloading the arms." [13]

This was hardly a crisis, as far as Begin was concerned. Upset with Galili's refusal to cooperate in the unloading of the "Altalena", Begin correctly estimated that the Irgun men were quite capable of taking care of this matter on their own. Little did he know of what lay ahead.

It was now dusk on June 21 when *Altalena* made its final approach towards Kfar Vitkin. A small boat appeared from the shore and Begin's familiar voice shouted a greeting of welcome to Lankin and the men standing by his side. A rope ladder was released and Begin stepped gingerly on to the firm deck of the *Altalena*. Within moments hundreds of volunteers surrounded the Irgun commander and greeted him with cheers and shouts of "Long live Begin!" The cheering continued until Begin returned to shore. ††

The time came to begin the unloading. There was a launch and two life boats on which crates could be ferried to the shore. On one of them Lankin, Fein and Stavsky were transported, together with several crates. Within minutes they reached the shore of Kfar Vitkin.

Lankin recalls: "Milling around among young men carrying crates were soldiers of Palmach—obviously kibbutzniks—who had ostensibly volunteered to help unload the *Altalena*. Menachem (Begin) introduced them to me reporting that they had promised to bring a few more boats at dawn to accelerate the slow pace of transferring the arms. We never saw them again. To this day, I am not sure whether or not they had really planned to help us or to spy on us." [14]

While the disembarkation was proceeding at a rather slow pace, some of the Irgun boys in the area managed to arrive at the pier. Some of them had stories to relate. They reported on scenes around Kfar Vitkin which hardly pointed towards an effort at cooperation, on behalf of the Israeli Army. There were reports of a young Irgun soldier being arrested, others detained and of a concentration of Israeli soldiers surrounding the area.

Suddenly, around noon, a note was delivered to the Irgun men on the pier. The note was signed by Dan Even, the area commander, and it read: "Units of the Israeli Defense Forces would employ all the weapons at their disposal unless all crates with arms on the *Altalena* were handed over within ten minutes." [15]

Moments later, two Israeli corvettes appeared. They stationed themselves west of the ship to bar its way to the open sea. Meanwhile. Israeli soldiers surrounded the beachhead.

During all this, Menachem Begin decided to collect all his men on the pier in order to explain to them that Meridor is presently negotiating with the Government and shortly everything will be straightened out. Before he uttered his first words, explosions sputtered the silence.

Lankin recalls: "Bullets whistled from all directions; mortars burst around us with deafening report. Menachem shouted for us all to disperse and take cover. He, Abrasha and several others decided to board the ship and sail for Tel Aviv. I joined them. As we pulled along side the *Altalena*, a rope ladder was lowered down to us and we climbed aboard. The launch was pulled aboard as well and the shooting ceased.

"In several minutes, we made radio contact with the corvettes. Their captains ordered us to proceed toward Tel Aviv and we answered that we would comply. As we adjusted our course, the two military vessels flanked us on the side of the open sea. Then suddenly, they issued new orders to change direction and head out to sea. What could this mean? There was no reason to take us further from Israel's shore unless our 'body guards' were planning to do away with us."

"We decided not to obey this new order and proceed instead toward Tel Aviv, choosing a point opposite Frishman Street to drop anchor". [16]

When the *Altalena* dropped anchor, it was some 150 meters off the beach with its bow stuck in a sandbar. At this time, the corvettes left the scene. The night suddenly became ominous and calm.

By daybreak June 23, the leadership left on board the *Altalena* included Begin, Lankin, Fein, Merlin, Stavsky, Germant and the professional crew. There was movement on the shore. Army units appeared on the beach and the rooftops of buildings and balconies. Anticipating a new assault on the ship, the Irgun leaders placed a loudspeaker on deck and appealed to those on shore to refrain from shooting.

In the meantime, the men left on board the *Altalena* began to load the crates on the only available launch. When the launch reached the shore, they piled the crates on the beach and began to return to the ship for an additional load.

Suddenly, a burst of fire from the beach, the roofs and the balconies began to rain down on the departing launch. Two men were immediately hit. The fire now was aimed at the *Altalena* directly. The bullets began to hit men on deck, several of whom were killed on the spot and some remained moaning from wounds.

Among the wounded was Bergson's able assistant, Shmuel Merlin. He was hit on the leg and his blood was leaking through his bandages and on to the mattress of his cot. Moments later, Abrasha Stavsky was brought to the same cabin and placed next to him, as he was struck by a bullet that had penetrated his knee bone. He lay there moaning quietly. Now, an Italian-American volunteer was being carried in from the deck. He was clinging to life, being hit by seven bullets in the chest. The few women on board bandaged the wounded, but some of them were dying.

Fire seemed to be reaching the holds of *Altalena* where crates of arms and ammunition were neatly piled in the holds.

"Raise the white flag!" commanded Captain Fein. "They must understand that they should stop firing at a ship loaded with ammunition!" ≠

It was one of the American volunteers who climbed up the rigging to hoist the white flag. "With relief" recalls Lankin, "we watched the white flag of surrender being hoisted on the mast. And still, the shooting and shelling continued". [17]

There was nothing left to be done but to abandon the burning ship. From the shore, a small rowboat, with Irgun men on board, approached the vessel. Some were shouting: "Where is the old man?" ## They came insisting on taking Begin safely to shore. Fein and Lankin in the meantime were doing exactly that— trying to persuade the commander to abandon ship. However, Begin was adamant. "Let others go first" he insisted. Finally, only after Lankin "pulled rank" by shouting: "I am the commander of this ship and I demand that you go ashore at once", did Begin agree. [18]

However, he would not leave until all wounded men were safely removed. It was now Lankin's and Fein's turn. The only problem was that Lankin did not know how to swim, but he was not about to worry the captain with such a "minor" detail. However, once in water and in spite of the life vest, Lankin began to sink. By now, Fein understood the problem and swam to Lankin's side.

"Suddenly", Lankin remembers, "Fein swam towards me and grabbed me shouting Hold onto my waist!" As he dragged me through the swell I watched how the explosives shook the *Altalena*. Then, someone pulled us out, put us in a car and drove us to the headquarters of the Irgun High Command." [19]

It was now all over. The survivors of the *Altalena* reached shore just as the ship started to explode. Most were met by jeeps which took them, naked and drenched, to Irgun headquarters. Felled in battle, on shore and at sea, were 83 casualties, including 14 dead! [20]

The Government held an emergency meeting which was assembled to approve the attack on the *Altalena*. The case was presented to the cabinet by Ben Gurion, who implied that the purpose of "Altalena" was to organize a putsch and take over the reins of the government. The Left majority in the Government readily accepted the pretext and approved "action." However, two ministers—Moshe Shapiro and Rabbi J. L. Fishman of the Mizrahi—resigned in protest, while the General Zionists opposed using force, claiming that the problems could have been settled without bloodshed.

Ignoring all protests, Ben Gurion ordered the final assault on the *Altalena* and when it was hit and destroyed, uttered his infamous comment: "Blessed be the gun that destroyed the *Altalena*!"

It was thus, at the climax of this tragedy, when Zion faced its ultimate test, that Begin addressed the Yishuv, using the Irgun radio for the last time.

Many books have been written on the "Altalena Affair". Strangely, not one of them was authored by a leftist, in defense of this tragic event, planned and executed by Ben Gurion and his Haganah commanders.

In most accounts, it was decisively proven that the Left's contention that the *Altalena* was brought with the purpose of overthrowing the Government by force, was nothing but a ridiculous fabrication, attested by dozens of examples indicating the complete absurdity of such charges. It would have sufficed to recall that the *Altalena* landed at Kfar Vitkin—a known base of the Left on the coast line of Israel. Likewise, the fact that on arrival at Kfar Vitkin, the Irgun instructed its volunteers from the *Altalena* to leave Kfar Vitkin on buses and proceed to their bases, without arms or ammunition, which were left behind on the shore and in the holds of the ship—ridicules the contention of a planned *putsch*.

Strangely however, no account of this tragic episode underlines the criminality of firing on a ship which had raised the internationally recognized white flag of surrender. This fact in itself indicates the black designs of the organizers of the *Altalena* assault. It was clearly a planned campaign to destroy physically, once and for all, both the Irgun as an organization and Menachem Begin, as its leader.

On the face of this summation, it may be appropriate to conclude this dark chapter with remarks uttered by Menachem Begin, as he commented on the criticism of his radio address to the nation, following the *Altalena* disaster . . .

"On that night in 1948 when the *Altalena* was destroyed, I spoke over the radio about the ship, its arms and its dead. I was moved to tears. And there were mighty heroes of all classes who listened to me from their armchairs and jeered at my 'soft emotionalism.' Let them jeer! There are tears of which no man need be ashamed; there are tears of which a man may be proud. Tears do not come only from the eyes; sometimes they well up, like blood, from the heart. There are tears that spring from sorrow; and there are tears that bring salvation.

"Whoever has followed my story knows that fate has not pampered me. From my earliest youth I have known hunger and been acquainted with sorrow. And often death has brooded over me, both in the Homeland and on alien soil. But for such things I have never wept. Only on the night when the State was proclaimed; and on the night of the *Altalena*...Truly there are tears of salvation as well as tears of grief. There are times when the choice is between blood and tears. Sometimes, as our revolt against the oppressor taught us, it is essential that blood should take the place of tears. And sometimes, as the *Altalena* taught us, it is essential that tears should take the place of blood. This should be remembered, particularly by those who shelled the *Altalena* and killed its men and shot at those, including wounded men, escaping from its flames.

"Let them not boast in their hearts of that act which 'somebody urged them to do' nor excuse themselves on his responsibility. Let them remember everything there is to remember, beginning with the secret hatching of the plan and ending with the last shell they fired into the burning and bleeding ship. If they remember this, perhaps they will understand the feeling of the man whose life they tried to take: and possibly they may understand that sometimes it is better that one man should pour tears from his heart over an abomination committed in Israel than that many, many should weep over its consequences...

"And so it came to pass that there was no fratricidal war in Israel to destroy the Jewish State before it was properly born. In spite of everything—there was no civil war!" [21]

Notes

* A feuilleton is a form of journalism that has never taken root in the American press. It was an art form highly developed in European Journalism and particularly by Jewish writers beginning with Heine and Borne down to Herzel and Jabotinsky. It is neither an essay, a short story, a topical article, nor a timely criticism. Rather, it is a combination of all of these.

** Shkolnik became Prime Minister Eshkol, succeeding David Ben Gurion in 1963

† From recollection of personal discussions between Lankin and the author in 1951

†† From recollection of personal discussions between Lankin and the author in 1951

Chapter 8

≠ The aforementioned paragraphs are based on an interview with Lankin, conducted by author in 1951

≠≠ Out of earshot, the Irgunists were in the habit of calling Begin "the old man".

1. *Rebel and Statesman* by J. Schechtman, Published by T. Yoseloff, NY 1956. Page 58
2. *Rebel and Statesman* by J. Schechtman, Published by T. Yoseloff, NY 1956. Pages 59-60
3. *To Win the Promised Land* by E. Lankin, Published by Benmir Books, San Francisco 1992. Page 260
4. *To Win the Promised* Land by E. Lankin. Page 261
5. *Genesis 1948* by Dan Durtzman. Published by the World Publishing Co. Cleveland, Ohio 1970, Pages 457-458
6. *Genesis 1948* by Kurtzman. Page 460
7. *Menachem Begin* by Hirschler and Eckman. Page 165
8. *Menachem Begin* by Hirschler and Eckman. Page 166
9. *Menachem Begin* by Hirschler and Eckman. Page 167
10. This is a quotation from Begin's speech on the Knesset floor as recorded in the *Divrei ha Knesset* (records of Israel's Parliament) session of January 7, 1952, Vol. 1. Pages 903-908
11. *Menachem Begin* by Hirshler and Eckman. Page 169
12. *Menachem Begin* by Hirshler and Eckman. Page 170
13. *Genesis 1948* by Dan Kurzman 1948. Page 465
14. *To Win the Promised Land* by Lankin. Pages 330-331
15. *To Win the Promised Land* by Lankin. Page 332
16. *To Win the Promised Land* by Lankin. Pages 333-334
17. *To Win the Promised Land* by Lankin. Page 338
18. *To Win the Promised Land* by Lankin. Page 340
19. *To Win the Promised Land* by Lankin. Page 341
20. *Genesis 1948* by Kurtzman. Pages 483-484
21. *The Revolt* by Menachem Begin. Del Publishing Co. New York. 1951. Pages 241-242.

Chapter 9
Twenty Years of Tears and Errors

After the *Altalena* tragedy, Ben Gurion and his Mapai-dominated government proceeded to rule the Jewish State with an iron hand. They were determined to install "socialism in our time" and to isolate their political opponents into irrelevance. To the best of their ability the Left attempted to deny any follower of Jabotinsky any position of prominence, be it in the sphere of politics, economy, diplomacy, education or even entertainment, the media or sport.

Although Ben Gurion aimed to keep the army clear of political controversy, it was not a coincidence that during the first 20 years of Mapai's rule, the army had no high ranking officer from supporters of the Right, be they members of the Herut Party or its youth movement—the Betar.

Besides the Government, the Histadrut (Federation of Labor) which was completely dominated by the Left, had a wide influence in every sphere of Israel's development. It was not only the largest trade union in the country; it also became the dominant proprietor of all major economic enterprises, including transportation, communications and the building industry.

The Histadrut proudly displayed slogans of international socialism and vigorously hoisted its red banner.

In Israel the concept of socialism became absolute, forbidding and dominant. It surpassed the general socialistic agenda of Europe, not to speak of the United States of America.

In America, where socialism was accepted as a national way of life from the days of President Franklin D. Roosevelt, it was limited to the basic philosophy of federalizing material aid to the nation's have-nots. It soon became a non-partisan issue and no longer divided Republicans from the Democrats. Capitalism, on the other hand, remained the widely acceptable, if not always preferable, method of economic practice. Competition and free marketing were and remain today the national trends of America's economy. They are equally embraced by the Left as well as the Right.

Therefore, Russia's socialist-communist doctrine of prescribed economics was never a serious threat to American capitalistic-socialism.

Not so in Israel.

Here, the Mapai leadership installed a system of dictatorial control over the national economy. This leftist approach to Israel's economic development placed an obvious taboo on outside participation in Israel's financial welfare. This was clearly expressed by the failures of some joint ventures with foreign capital, when the Histadrut demanded and received at least 51% of participation shares. Furthermore, potential investors were turned away by these efforts to control, dictate and rule. As a result, the Israeli pound devalued daily, inflation galloped and the national state of economy reached a dangerous decline.

In the meantime, obligated by its basic commitment to Jewry as a whole, Israel was in the process of absorbing more than a million refugees fleeing extinction in a variety of Moslem lands with significant Jewish populations.

Mass dissatisfaction of the citizens of Israel was stifled by the ruling Mapai party through a totalitarian control of people's income, employment and promotions.

This was the prevailing mood in the country in 1951 when Israel reached its first major internal crisis: The reparations controversy.

Throughout the year, Dr. Nahum Goldman of the Jewish Congress, sitting in America, assumed leadership in championing the cause of German reparations to the Jewish People. The subject was handled in two areas—"private" reparations to the survivors and heirs of the Holocaust victims and "State to State" reparations from Germany to Israel, as an expression of moral responsibility for Hitler's devastation of Jewish limb and property during the Nazi reign.

Ben Gurion and Israel's Left were in accord with Goldman's "compensation agenda" and supported the idea of "State to State" reparations to be negotiated between the governments of Israel and the German Republic.

In violently emotional opposition to any direct negotiations between the two governments, Begin led the Herut Party in an all-embracing campaign against "betraying our honor in negotiating with the murderers of our People".

Many supported the movement to oppose negotiations of State to State reparations between Israel and Germany. There were those in both camps who sympathized with Begin's anti-reparations arguments. It may have very well happened that a national vote (a referendum) on the issue would have supported Begin against Ben Gurion and, indirectly, the Right against the Left.

Tragically for himself, Begin made a significant political error by crossing the border of his own line of national solidarity. In one of his major anti-reparation speeches, he went too far. Invigorated by the heat of his own rhetoric during the final Knesset debate on the issue, Begin, pointing at Ben Gurion, declared, "When you aimed your guns at us and I was standing on the deck of the *Altalena* as it burned, I gave the order: 'No. Do not answer fire with fire.' Today, I give the order: 'Yes!'" [1]

Ben Gurion's immediate reaction was to accuse Begin of taking "the first steps toward the destruction of democracy in Israel."

Perhaps the most poignant error of judgment on Begin's part was in the solitude of his decision. If he would have given himself time to reconsider or consult with a wider circle within his Party, he may have well refrained from these dangerous and provocative declarations.

As it came about, nothing serious resulted from this, aside from the fact that a dozen or so former members of the Irgun were only too anxious to return to the romantic and challenging days of the "Revolt".

Among these was a future speaker of the Knesset—a 29 year old Dachau survivor, Dov Shilansky, who was caught carrying a briefcase with a bomb set to go off within moments of his arrival at the Israeli Ministry of Foreign Affairs. As a result Shilansky was tried and sentenced to 21 months in jail.

Although Herut as such had no connection with the Shilansky affair, the Israeli newspapers, at the time, concluded that Shilansky was part of a dissident rump of the Irgun that believed Begin had erred in disbanding the underground.

In spite of the fact that it was Begin's rhetoric that keynoted the revived "underground", he personally seems to have avoided involvement in or knowledge of specific acts of violence. [2]

Gradually, the furor over the reparations subsided enough to allow the citizens of Israel to concentrate on a cause of a more immediate importance: Survival!

Retroactively, it would be fair to note that in spite of some disastrous effects of Begin's anti-reparations campaign; it was not a total fiasco. History will be obliged to record that there was a significant bi-partisan opposition to the decision of negotiating "with the murderers of our People". The fact that the Government of Israel shied away from holding a referendum, adds credit to the contention that a majority of Israelis may have opposed the Government on this issue.

In the meantime, continuous attacks on the civilian population by the organized terrorist gangs stimulated the Right to demand action from the Government and the armed forces of Israel.

This campaign encouraged by daily reports of Israeli civilian casualties, led Ben Gurion to consider favorably the possibility of a "preventive war," in a covert alliance with England and France.

On October 28, 1956 Ben Gurion summoned Menachem Begin to his home in Tel Aviv and informed him of his decision to invade Sinai the next day. Begin's emotional response was: "I applaud your courageous decision. Rest assured of our support". [3]

Once again the nation stood united and the Israeli soldier on the front lines was being supported by all citizens of Israel as well as by the vast majority of world Jewry.

Regretfully, once again, the blessed days of Zion united were not meant to last.

Under enormous and combined pressures of the United States and the Soviet Union, Ben Gurion retreated from Sinai, relying on U.S. President Dwight Eisenhower's assurances to keep the Suez Canal open to Israeli shipping. Likewise, the Sinai was to be neutralized by a contingent of UN forces, providing Israel with a promise of support by the World Organization.

The Right, led by Begin and his Herut Party, opposed Israel's retreat from the Sinai and discounted the "empty guarantees" of the United Nations' organization.

It took less than five years, before it became obvious to all concerned, that Israel has been misled not only by the United Nations but also by President Eisenhower and his pro-Arab Administration.

By 1967, Egypt's President Gamel Abdel Nasser, armed by the Soviets and supported by the majority members of UN's General Assembly, declared openly his intention to "wipe Israel off the map of the world."

Of course, the Suez remained closed to Israeli shipping. Nasser ordered the UN forces in Sinai to leave and proceeded to blockade the Straits of Tiran, thus denying Israel its gateway to the Orient.

Some months before this ominous development began to take shape as a concrete threat to Israel's survival; Ben Gurion left his Mapai Party and retreated to Sde Boker—a kibbutz in the Negev, not far from Beersheba. Levi Eshkol was chosen as a new head of the party, thus automatically becoming the next Prime Minister of Israel.

This internal Party upheaval was developing for several years. It began in early 1954, when Ben Gurion decided to take a long vacation in Sde Boker. His duties of Prime Minister, at the time, were assigned to Moshe Sharett, while he personally selected Pinhas Lavon to replace him as Minister of Defense.

While Ben Gurion was in Sde Boker, leaders of Mapai continued to make constant "pilgrimages" to him. Nor did he hesitate to conduct affairs of the State from his "temporary retirement".

It was during this period (1954—1955) that the famous "Lavon Affair" exploded. The "affair" was a major security blunder "related to an espionage mission in Egypt in 1954 (disastrous in its very conception, to say nothing of its execution)". [4]

As a result, Ben Gurion returned, first to the Defense Ministry, and soon afterwards to the premiership. Sharett returned to the Foreign Ministry, but the relationship between him and Ben Gurion were soured.

Of course Lavon was in no position to continue. He resigned—a broken and bitter man.

Then, six years later, the "Lavon Affair" erupted anew. "This time," writes Golda Meir in her memoirs *My Life*, "it turned into a major political scandal with the most tragic after effects inside Mapai itself. It upset and confused the Israeli public for months, and it led, indirectly, to my own break with Ben Gurion and to his second and final resignation as Prime Minister." [5]

In 1960 Lavon claimed that during the initial inquiry into the scandal, false evidence had been given and many documents had been forged. Ben Gurion, in turn, demanded a new inquiry into the matter, while leaders of the Mapai Party were opposed to "washing the linen in public." Devastated, Ben Gurion returned to Sde Boker. This time for good.

Rejected by his comrades of many years, Ben Gurion, backed by his young lieutenants Moshe Dayan and Shimon Peres left Mapai to inaugurate a new political party called "Rafi." Eshkol became the new Prime Minister of Israel and Golda Meir took over as Minister of Foreign Affairs.

While the enemy was sending its Fedayeen terrorists across Israel's borders and announcing to the world at large that the goal was total liquidation of the State of Israel, the World Organization and its pivotal members such as the USA, Soviet Union, Britain and France not only remained totally passive to the unfolding tragedy, but also displayed a clear policy of appeasement towards the Arab threats of aggression.

The Left Government of Israel, at the same time, instead of consolidating and uniting all Jews of Israel and the world at large, continued its obsessive absorption with internal intrigues and power politics.

The closer Israel approached its hour of destiny, the more disenchanted became the overall mood and spirit of Israel's Jewish population. The economy was in shatters, immigration reached a standstill and the mass evacuation developed into a severe crisis threatening an internal collapse. The jesting slogan of the day became: "The last one out of the Lydda airport—please turn off the lights!"....

From the days of Theodore Herzel and the first Zionist Congress, Zionism had seen no darker days. During the two decades of Israel's struggles, war, hunger and severe isolation—this was the blackest period and its darkest hour.

Jews always had enemies, but they knew how to face up to them and emerge as survivors. The Jewish people also knew how to combat isolation and indifference of the world around.

The uniqueness of the impending catastrophe was in the fact that Zionists, both in Israel and in the Diaspora, had finally realized that they were being led to a dead-end. Worse—that Zionism has been misguided by foreign philosophies of internationalism, intrigue, fratricide and hunger for power. All these weapons of the socio-communistic Left—had now brought Israel to the brink of destruction.

But while Zion cried and Zionists panicked, the military genius of the State of Israel was at work.

Moshe Dayan, presently out of the Government and out of the Mapai Party, leaning on his popularity and military reputation, asked for and received permission to visit the front lines of Israel and to report back on his findings. Dayan's main concern was to have Israel strike the first blow. Especially now that "causus belli" has been established (Egyptian take over of the Straits of Tiran), it was essential to take the initiative.

In his book *Story of my Life*, Dayan notes: "I was convinced that the most important step for us now was to meet the challenge of Egyptian might and defeat it. It would be catastrophic if Israel were to be seized by hysterical fear and start banging on the doors of the Big Powers, begging them to come to her rescue. Such an entreaty would immediately invite 'conditions' and all this when in fact, as I firmly believed; we were capable of putting the Egyptians to rout." [6]

Within the ruling Mapai Party, the pacifists and the "internationalists" prevented Eshkol from bringing in a cabinet of National Unity. Abba Eban, till the last moment opposed the "first strike" and opted to rely on American help in the event of an attack. Golda Meir too sided with the anti-first strike majority. Eshkol was not a man of decisions. He wavered and negotiated with the opposing sides to prevent a break down in the Government.

It was in this atmosphere that the nation was called to listen to the radio address of the Prime Minister. It was a disaster. Even Eshkol's solid supporter and friend, Golda Meir, remarked, ". . . he spoke hesitantly and without any flair, when what the country wanted was more dynamic leadership." [7]

Moshe Dayan, who often found excuses for Eshkol's inability to make decisions, commented in his autobiography: "The Prime Minister faltered and bumbled throughout his address, stumbling over the words. (I learned later that the speech had been hurriedly prepared and hastily typed with many errors and Eshkol had not had time to go over it before being rushed to the microphones). What the public heard were the halting phrases of a man unsure of himself." [8]

This was indeed the 12th hour for Israel. Nasser was issuing his daily threats proclaiming that Israel will be taken off the map momentarily, while the UN seemed to be completely disinterested in the consequences. Israel's only true ally, the USA, advised caution and promised to help in the event of an attack. The Left majority in Eshkol's cabinet supported the policy of "wait and see". But the People on the street, backed by the usually pro-government media, openly insisted on the establishment of a wall-to-wall government of national unity and the return of Dayan to head the Ministry of Defense.

The Right's position, as represented by Menachem Begin of the Herut Party, favored an immediate return of Ben Gurion to the helm and the appointment of Dayan as Minister of Defense. Herut supported immediate action and was prepared to demonstrate national unity by joining Ben Gurion's cabinet if called on to do so.

Eshkol continued to hesitate. He personally accepted the idea of a government of national unity and even of Dayan replacing him as Minister of Defense. But he would not accept the notion of sitting in the same cabinet with Ben Gurion. To those who insisted, he proclaimed- "These two horses can not pull together".

Nevertheless, Begin decided to call on Ben Gurion who was lying ill in his apartment in Tel Aviv. According to Begin's biographer, Ned Temko, "Begin saw the mission as an exercise in patriotism, putting nation above party. However, when Begin proposed that the ex-prime minister lead the country into Sinai, Ben Gurion suggested that the army simply 'take Sharm el-Sheikh and wind the crisis down'. It thus became clear to Begin that the "old man" did not have much grasp of the situation on the ground. He subsequently had no choice but to abandon his campaign to bring back Ben Gurion." [9]

In the meantime, pressure was mounting. The nation was clamoring for action. Eshkol could no longer ignore the situation by appeasing his far-Left majority. As a result, he invited Begin for consultations. During the meeting Begin again proposed the creation of a Government of National Unity. He further insisted that the Prime Minister resign as Defense Minister in favor of Moshe Dayan.

Levy Eshkol finally accepted Begin's proposal and invited Dayan to succeed him as Minister of Defense. He also invited Menachem Begin and Yosef Sapir (of the Herut-Liberal Bloc) to join the cabinet along with Dayan. [10]

On June 5. 1967 the Israeli armed forces went into action. The war lasted six days. As a result Jerusalem, Judea. Samaria and Gaza were liberated. The Golan Hights was conquered. And Israel exalted in the victory and prayed that permanent peace might soon follow. . . .

Notes

1. *To Win or to Die* by Ned Temko, New York 1987. Page 137
2. *To Win or to Die* by Ned Temko. Page 139
3. *To Win or to Die* by Ned Temko. Page 144
4. *My Life* by Golda Meir. Keystone Press, Israel 1975. Page 288
5. *My Life* by Golda Meir. Page 289
6. *Story of My Life* by Moshe Dayan. Israel 1976. Page 330
7. *My Life* by Golda Meir. Page 362
8. *Story of My Life* by Moshe Dayan. Page 333
9. *To Win or to Die* by Ned Temko. Published by Morrow & Co, New York 1987
10. *Begin: A Portrait* by Hurwitz. Published by BBB Washington 1994. Pages 65-67

Part 2

Political Upheaval in Zionism

Chapter 10
Blood and Tears—Victories and "Earthquake"

The Six Day War did more than reunite Jerusalem with the People of Israel and world Jewry at large. It forcefully underlined the realism behind Jabotinsky's concept of biblical Eretz Israel.

On the other hand, this war of liberation of Judea, Gaza and Samaria as well as the unification of Jerusalem as Israel's ancient and modern capital, symbolized the errors and blindness of the false prophets of appeasement who advocated co-existence with the Arabs at the cost of Israel's most sacred possessions.

But this was not all. The Six Day War also would be remembered as a last frontier of the Left's domination of Zionism. The days of Mapai's control of Zion's dreams and of the State of Israel's future, were now coming to a close. Marxism of the far left, together with its ideological goal of *uravnilovka* (equalization), were on the verge of bankruptcy not only in Israel but also in the womb of its creation—the Soviet Union.

The days when Jabotinsky's disciples were ostracized from leadership of Zionist and Jewish State affairs, were no more. Ben Gurion was ousted from the helm by his own Party. Begin, on the other hand, was now enjoying recognition and a status of honor within the Government and among the citizens of Israel.

Immediately following Eshkol's death, Golda Meir of Mapai was chosen to lead the Party. Thus, automatically, she became Prime Minister of the existing Government of National Unity.

The first serious test of this Government came with the arrival of the American Secretary of State, William Rogers, whose task was to negotiate Israel's retreat to the 1948 borders in return for "peace".

The typical attitude of appeasement of the past Government of Israel was now stymied by the Herut (Gahal) presence in the Cabinet. Begin led the opposition against surrendering any territories of Eretz Israel, as well as the Golan Heights, predicated not only on Israel's biblical and historic rights but also on those areas' strategic importance.

Although the sharp political divisions remained, a new day was dawning on the political horizon of the Jewish State. However, world Jewry would be slow in following this trend, especially the "liberal minded" Jewry in the United States.

Not all changes were to imply an improvement. Although Zionism persisted, some Zionists began to abandon it. This was especially true within the ranks of the Jewish Leftists. Many followers of Ben Gurion and believers in socialistic doctrines of Mapai were disillusioned and disenchanted.

Some lost their political compasses and began searching for others. Their youth, on the other hand, found their own causes within the general outlines of their generation's "rebellion." Many Israeli youths strove to duplicate their western contemporaries both in Europe and in the United States. It was this latter category that began to shape the contours of modern liberalism.

Universally, the rebellious generation in the west enthusiastically embraced pacifism, internationalism and wholesale appeasement. It expounded tolerance for everyone but their opponents. Since much of this new ideology came from the disillusioned and devastated leftists, the rebellious generation adopted the basic leftists' positions such as socialism through equalization and internationalism through appeasement.

As a result of this trend, advocates of modern liberalism were able to proselytize among the discouraged members of the bankrupt Zionist-socialist camp, in the State of Israel. On the other hand, within the United States, this new "liberalism" penetrated and "conquered" the Democratic Party of the Roosevelt-Kennedy vintage, thus hijacking the classical liberalism of the past.

In the United States, the new "liberal" (read: leftist) movement began to develop during the catastrophic period of the Vietnam War. In Israel, it raised its head immediately following the Six Day War and began to grow in direct proportion to the gradual decline of the Mapai Party and all its fabricated satellites.

However, at the time of negotiations between Mrs. Meir's Government and the US Secretary of State Rogers, this "liberalism" was in its embryo state, hardly noticed by either the press or the citizenship in Israel. Nevertheless, it was clearly felt within the leadership of Mapai, including Mrs. Meir and the remnants of its "old" generation.

No doubt, it was on Meir's mind when she became determined to cling to her shaky coalition of national unity. In fact, she went as far as to offer Begin's "Gahal" four additional cabinet portfolios in an attempt to keep them in the Unity Government. More than this, "Mrs. Meir agreed to omit specific mention of returning the West Bank in exchange for peace in her new Government's platform." [1]

On December 10, 1969, the American Secretary of State announced a joint bid with Moscow for Mideast peace. However, Prime Minister Meir indicated to Begin that she favored rejecting the US move. As a direct result of this firm attitude, a new Government was formed with Begin and three other members of "Gahal" (Herut-General Zionist Bloc) joining Mapai in a new Government of National Unity.

But, once again, the utopia of a united front did not last long.

This was the time when the War of Attrition was raging ferociously. Both Egypt and Syria were fully re-equipped by the Soviet Union, which more than compensated for their losses during the Six Day War.

By 1971 it became clear to U.S. President Richard Nixon that Rogers' State Department was dangerously leaning towards cooperation with the Soviets in pressuring for Israel's return to the borders of 1967. To counter balance this trend Nixon began to rely on his National Security Advisor—Dr. Henry Kissinger. In his book *Years of Upheaval*, Kissinger recalls: "Late in 1971, Nixon began shifting responsibility (regarding the Middle East) to me. He was afraid that the State Department's bent for abstract theories might lead to propose plans that would arouse opposition from all sides."[2]

Thus, when Rogers came to Israel, he was pressuring Golda Meir in the name of the State Department and the Russians rather than on behalf of either President Nixon or his Advisor on National Security Affairs, Dr. Kissinger.

This obvious and well known conflict between the White House and the State Department should have been seriously considered by the Prime Minister of Israel, as well. Surprisingly, it was not.

In her book *My Life*, Mrs. Meir touched on her conflict with Begin, during the anticipated Rogers' visit to Jerusalem. She wrote: "I tried to explain to Begin that we won't have any cease-fire unless we also accept some of the less favorable conditions. And what is more, we won't get any arms from America."[3]

This approach was based on poor judgment and misunderstanding of the true atmosphere within the American Administration at the time. The prime minister of Israel should have known that the overtly pro-Israel Congress would act to prevent any bullying of Israel by the State Department on this crucial issue of surrendering territory before peace was seriously negotiated.

Not surprisingly, Menachem Begin rejected withdrawal prior to negotiations. And when Pinhas Sapir (Mrs. Meir's Minister of Finance) proposed that Begin and "Gahal" ministers be given the right to vote against the proposal in the Cabinet and the Knesset, he firmly rejected this compromise as a "dishonest act." As a result, "the next morning Begin tendered his resignation from the Government, with Gahal ministers following suit, some of them most reluctantly."[4]

In the meantime, Secretary Rogers' pressure on Israel continued. So did the flow of arms, including new land to air missiles, supplied by Russia to both Egypt and Syria.

During this period, quite unexpectedly, Nasser passed away and was replaced by Anwar Sadat.

Terror strikes on Israel continued with no interruption. But the general population was still bathing in the sunshine of confidence inspired by the sensational victory in the Six Day War.

However, on deeper examination, the situation reflected a less attractive scenario. Israel's Labor Parties were consumed with internal upheavals. "With Eshkol gone," wrote Ned Temko, "Mrs. Meir was under fire from Rafi pretenders to her throne. The country was strained with tensions between rich and poor, the Labor aristocracy and a frustrated middle-class."⁵ Aside from former Rafi comrades who wished to inherit the leadership of the Party, a new element appeared on the horizon. It too came from the ranks of Israel's Left, but claimed as its only declared goal: "achievement of peace at all cost." This new element began to conduct its various activities under an unpretentious slogan of "Peace Now." Soon they became the core of Israel-bashing appeasers—not too different from the "new liberals," of America, who were fermenting there since the war in Vietnam.

On the other side of the coin, the Gahal in Israel was under a shadow of its own rebellion brought forth by the maverick politician-soldier Ezer Weizman. He was a nephew of Israel's first President, Chaim Weizmann. However, in his youth he was schooled in Mapai's political thought. He reached his pinnacle of fame as a highly successful commander of Israel's victorious Air Force.

Gen. Weizman gradually became attracted to Begin's and Gahal's ideology and agreed to join forces with them in order to "assure the sanctity of Israel's liberated lands".

In an overenthusiastic welcome Gahal appointed him one of their four ministers in the Government. Ironically, this did not last long. Soon, Begin withdrew Gahal from the coalition and Weizman, reluctantly, left his ministerial chair before having a chance to "warm" it.

Now, in opposition, Weizman began to plot a "revolt" within the Herut Party of the Gahal Union, by ridding it of the "old guard" surrounding Begin and substituting it with his own followers and the young generation of the Party, itching to replace the "old faithful" from the days of the underground's "fighting family".

Sensing an open challenge, Menachem Begin addressed the Herut convention of 1972, in a major oration before a full-house audience of party faithful. "By the time the convention voted Ezer was in no position to appoint anybody as anything," according to Temko.⁶

Weizman, contrary to his norm, accepted the defeat gracefully and thus remained in the party leadership. He was rewarded for this by being appointed chairman of the committee for national elections scheduled to take place in 1973.

In the meantime General Ariel Sharon, also of the Six Day War fame, became disillusioned with the policies of the Labor Government. He too was adamant in his belief that Israel should remain on the land liberated and conquered during the Six Day War. After joining the Liberal (General Zionist) Party and thus becoming an important voice in the Gahal Union, Sharon approached Begin and the former members of Rafi, (who refused to return to Mapai) with a proposition for a wider union against Labor for the approaching elections.

By mid September 1973 a new political bloc was born. It included the Herut Party, the General Zionists (Liberals), plus the Land of Israel Movement, the State List and the Free Center (a group that had broken away from Herut and now returned as a separate entity). This new bloc was named: The Likud.

Suddenly, Israel was hit with a "Pearl Harbor" of its own. On Yom Kippur, the holiest day of the Jewish year, Israel was attacked by Syria in the north and Egypt on the south. Unknown at the time to both the aggressor and its victim, this war, like no other would become a threat to Israel's very existence.

On the first day of the war Israeli public influenced by the self-serving assurances of the Government, were still under the illusion that its arms were invincible and its ability unmatched. . . .

Contrary to these illusions or rather, because of them, the Yom Kippur War produced grave consequences. Some 3,000 Israeli soldiers lost their lives. Thousands more were wounded and maimed. For the first time in its short history, there was panic. Panic in the cabinet, panic in the High Command and panic on the street. The main blunder was attributed to the leadership which failed to see and was too slow to react. To her credit, Prime Minister Meir admits her grave error as she noted in her autobiography: "It does not matter what logic dictated. It matters only that I, who was so accustomed to making decisions and who did make them throughout the war failed to make that one decision. It wasn't a question of feeling guilty. I too, can rationalize and tell myself that in the face of such total certainty on the part of our foremost military men—it would have been unreasonable of me to have insisted on a call up. But I knew that I should have done so, and I shall live with that terrible knowledge for the rest of my life. I will never be the person I was before the Yom Kippur War."[7]

And neither would her Party, the Left nor the entire House of Israel. . . .

The victory of the Yom Kippur War was anything but a foregone conclusion. Not only was the Israeli Government and its military chiefs convinced of Israel's invincibility, but their arrogance influenced the American administration and its military intelligence to be totally mesmerized with its self-confidence. As a result, when Israel's military supplies dropped dangerously low, Meir had a difficult time convincing the Nixon Administration of the need and the extreme urgency for additional military supplies.

However, when Israel's situation became clear, President Nixon took personal charge, with the assistance of Henry Kissinger, to order immediate re-supply of all requested equipment ranging from ammunition to tanks, planes and missiles.

On the field, Gen. Sharon earned the title of "the man of the hour." His daring and brilliant crossing of the Suez helped surround the entire Third Army of Egypt and bring the aggressors to the negotiating table.

Here again, American pressure and Israeli Government's reluctance to stand firm, resulted in a total loss of Israel's tragically earned military and political advantages.

The public in the Jewish State began to realize that they were let down not only in war preparedness but also in post-war political maneuvering. Little wonder that the elections, following on the heels of the Yom Kippur War reduced the Labor membership in the Knesset by nine parliamentarians and enlarged the Likud contingent to 39. Nevertheless, with a coalition of 51 votes in the new Knesset, Golda Meir was able to form a shaky Government, heavily relying on the support of a few Arab members of the Knesset.

In spite of her tiny majority in the elections, Golda Meir was visibly unpopular, as a result of the tragic war and the poorly conducted negotiations which neutralized the victory. Ted Nemko, describing the situation wrote: "Nearly everywhere Golda Meir or Moshe Dayan went, in the months after the war, they met the venom of the crowd. Bereaved parents hooted 'murderer!'"[8] All this had little effect. But when an official inquiry commission questioned the government's handling of the war, Golda and Dayan saw little choice but to share the blame. As a result, both resigned.

The reins of the Government now fell into the hands of Gen. Itzhak Rabin, who outvoted his Labor Party rival by a small percentage of votes. The competitor was the former co-founder of Rafi—Shimon Peres, who had been given the post of Minister of Defense. The days of Left's domination of Israel's politics were coming to an end.

The Likud, in the meantime, was preparing itself for the elections scheduled to take place in May 1977. The campaign was bitter. The Left was severely criticized for its tragic errors in both war and peace, while on the Right, it was Menachem Begin personally that became (again) the brunt of every conceivable denunciation including such terms as "fascist", "dictator" and "a clown".

In the only pre-election debate between Rabin and Begin, the latter outstripped the former in every argument, be it on the subject of domestic or political perspective. Some called it a "massacre." Harry Hurwitz, in his usually mild manner, remarked: "If points had been awarded, there was little doubt that Begin had won. It was the triumph of the experienced and polished statesman".[9]

The election results were classified as a "catastrophe", a "revolution" and an "earthquake", depending from whom the comments were being elicited.

But there was no doubt that the average man on the street would be in agreement with Mrs. Rose Schaffer of Jerusalem, who wrote in the "Jerusalem Post": "Israel has taken, with its last gasp of healthy breath, the first step of regeneration. If, as a bereaved mother, I could be said to have felt since the Yom Kippur War something akin to jubilation, it came on learning that the Labor Alignment had finally been toppled from its high and mighty chair of omnipotence. I trust and pray that our new leaders, whoever they may be, will gradually, if laboriously, lift Israel to the pinnacle of idealism it should never have fallen from". [10]

For the first time since the 17th Zionist Congress in 1931, when Labor took control of the World Zionist Movement, Jabotinsky's followers were elevated to lead the nation and given a mandate to govern the State of Israel.

This was the time of the total collapse of Socialist Zionism and a time of vindication of monism within the movement of Jewish national rejuvenation as advanced by Zeev Jabotinsky.

The old regime, hoisting red flags and influenced by Marxist ideology, would never return. Israel's Labor parties suddenly disintegrated into secondary goals, often borrowing from America's newfound Left-liberalism, which openly heralded the concepts of equalization, internationalism and appeasement.

Whereas in America, this New Liberalism of the Left succeeded in hijacking the Democratic Party, in Israel, it only managed to penetrate, weaken and destroy the cohesion and unity of the Labor Party, as a whole.

This Movement began with a call for concessions on behalf of peace (The Peace-Now Movement) and it gradually degenerated into a radical anti-Zionist political Party called "Meraz", which was dominated alternatively by Yossi Beilin and Yossi Sarid.

The Meraz Party rejected religious orthodoxy, revised Jewish contemporary history and promoted the theory of Israel's enemies regarding the status of "occupied" land and oppression of Arab rights.

The bulk of the Labor Party, while remaining within the original framework, adopted the basic concepts of Meraz followers. They stayed in the Party ranks while proceeding to inseminate new Liberal ideals into the disintegrating body of the socialist Party of old. All this became rather obvious after the electoral defeat suffered by the Left during the 1977 elections.

In the meantime however, following the Yom Kippur War period, the ruling Labor Party, under the leadership of Itzhak Rabin, faced a discontented public, fed up with Left's domination, corruption and lack of stamina to lead the nation out of isolation, economic disaster and moral morass.

On the other hand, Begin's Likud was now strengthened with the additional membership of the newly organized "Land of Israel" Movement, comprised of elements disenchanted with Labor, as well as of a scattered variety of Religious Parties and groupings.

Another boost to Begin came when sharp internal criticism of Labor's leadership found expression in the defection of such prominent Mapai "stars" as Professor Yigal Yadin, Meir Amit and General Aharon Yariv. These and others left "Mapai" to form a "Democratic Movement for Change."

The "earthquake" elections of 1977 voted Labor out and installed Begin and his Likud as the new Government of Israel.

Another significant change occurred in the position previously held by some Religious Parties in the country. These included the most powerful, known as the "National Religious Party." It was always recognized by friend and foe alike that the Religious element in the Country supported the Left in order to maintain a firm grip on religious affairs in general and education in particular. Their political sentiments were always closer to those held by the nationalists. It was only natural that the National Religious Party would enthusiastically join Begin's Coalition Government.

And thus it finally happened. On the next day following the election victory, the followers of Jabotinsky massed at the grave of their venerable leader and mentor to hear Begin "report" that his ideas prevailed, his call has been answered and his political credo had been accepted by the vast majority of the Nation.

Other than that, there was no gloating among Begin's followers and admirers. There were no recriminations and no calls for vengeance. On the contrary, Begin spoke of unity in the nation and brotherhood within the entire Jewish family, throughout the world. On appearing before his comrades late at night—after the election results were announced—he quoted Abraham Lincoln: "This was not a time to settle scores. It was a time to bind up wounds—not a time for malice, but for charity."

"In fact," writes Hurwitz in his biography of Begin, "from the moment he ascended to the post of Prime Minister, Begin's leadership style was characterized by a degree of statesmanship and respect rarely seen in modern politics. Shimon Peres, who became leader of the Opposition, was accorded all the respect and recognition due to his office and his status in the parliamentary life of the Country. He was given an honored place at official functions and addressed by the Prime Minister as 'my friend, the leader of the opposition'. When Peres made his first speech as leader of the opposition, in the debate following the presentation of Begin's first Cabinet, the Prime Minister complimented him and then brought the House down when he added: 'You made a good speech—not as good as the previous leader of the opposition—but don't worry, you'll have lots of time to learn and improve." [11]

Indeed the mood and the spirit in the whole Country seemed to change to the better. There was no more hate, no more vengeance and no more tears. . . .

Would the Left allow this spirit of unity and brotherhood continue to shine on the population of Israel? Would the atmosphere of goodwill continue to lift all Israelis and all of the world's Jewry "to the pinnacle of idealism"?

It would not take long to discover the answers to these questions. And these answers would bring more divisions among Jewry and more tears to Zion.

Notes

1. *To Win or to Die* by Ned Temko. Published by William Morrow Co. Page 174
2. *Years of Upheaval* by H. Kissinger. Publ. 1982. Page 196
3. *My Life* by Golda Meir. Page 385
4. *Begin: A Portrait* by Harry Hurwitz. Page 73
5. *To Win or to Die* by Ned Temko. Page 184
6. *To Win or to Die* by Ned Temko. Page 182
7. *My Life* by Golda Meir. Page 425
8. *To Win or to Die* by Ned Temko. Page 188
9. *Begin: A Portrait* by Hurwitz. Page 89
10. *Begin: A Portrait* by Hurwitz. Page 88
11. *Begin: A Portrait* by Hurwitz. Page 104

Chapter 11
Siding with the Enemy in Peace and in War

The "honeymoon" of Begin's premiership lasted longer than originally predicted. It was capped by the historic peace treaty signed between Begin and Anwar Sadat of Egypt. These were good days for Israel—days of fraternity, goodwill and general acclamation.

Almost immediately following the establishment of a Likud-led coalition Government, Begin launched his relentless campaign to bridge the financial and social gaps between the haves and have-nots of Israel. The campaign centered on a successful program of recovery among the predominantly "backward" elements, mostly immigrants from African countries.

Likewise, the coalition Government of the Likud began to concentrate on a campaign designed to bring Jews from the Soviet Union to Israel. Eventually, with powerful support of the United States, hundreds of thousands of Jews from Russia were able to leave the Soviet Union and settle in Israel.

These Jews traveled to Austria from where they were brought by specially chartered El-Al planes to the Ben Gurion airport in Israel.

On the diplomatic arena, Begin succeeded in creating an atmosphere of understanding and mutual respect not only with the government in the United States but also in Britain, where he was welcomed as an honored guest of Prime Minister James Callaghan.

However, the most significant gesture of the newly elected Prime Minister was not in the field of diplomacy but rather in a spectacular show of the high morality of Israel's new regime.

Begin's first official act was when he decided to admit to Israel 66 stranded Vietnamese refugees, rescued by an Israeli freighter off the coast of Vietnam. When the Israeli captain of "Yuvali" first sighted the boat, it was close to sinking. Ships of four other nations were observed passing the refugees, but declined to offer assistance. As soon as Begin was contacted, he immediately gave orders to pick up the refugees and bring them to Israel.

When U.S. President Jimmy Carter complimented the Prime Minister of Israel on this humanitarian gesture, Begin replied: "We have not forgotten the sufferings of our own people." The Vietnamese refugees were flown to the

Jewish State, where more than half of them, settled, received work permits, pocket money, toys for children and ample supplies of fish, rice and vegetables which the Vietnamese regard as staple food. [1]

During the first six months after his election, Begin devoted much time to visiting a variety of capitals of friendly and not so friendly countries in Europe. Among these, a potentially historic visit to Rumania took place. During this visit Begin spoke candidly with Rumania's president, Nicolae Ceausescu, regarding possible solutions to the Arab-Israeli confrontation. It was in the midst of these discussions that Begin told Ceausescu that he would welcome a personal meeting with Egypt's president Anwar Sadat.

A month after Begin's visit to Rumania, Sadat of Egypt came to pay his respects to Ceausescu in Bucharest. The two men discussed Begin's conversation with the President, especially his desire to meet and converse with Sadat.

Shortly following his visit to Rumania, on November 9, 1977, Sadat announced to his People's Assembly (the Egyptian Parliament) that he was ready to go "to the ends of the world" in search of peace. "Israel," Sadat continued, "will be astonished to hear me saying before you now that I am ready to go to their House, to the Knesset itself, and to talk to them so that there might be peace in the Middle East at last." [2]

In reply Begin delivered a radio address to the people of Egypt, saying: "Much blood was shed on both sides. The time had come for the Peoples of Egypt and Israel to live together in friendship and cooperation." [3]

Three days later, Sadat was interviewed by the world renowned American journalist, Walter Cronkite. In this interview the Egyptian president announced his readiness to go to Israel within a week, if he would receive an official invitation from Begin. Such an invitation was not long in coming. By the very next day it was transmitted to Sadat through the courtesy of the U.S. Ambassador in Israel, Samuel Louis.

As a result, Sadat's plane landed in Lod at 8:03 p.m., greeted by fanfare and a 21 gun salute, as the army band played first the Egyptian national anthem and then the Hatiqvah—the national anthem of Israel.

Thus, the road to Camp David in the USA and the final ceremony of a peace treaty between Egypt and Israel was paved.

In spite of demonstrations and protests, vilifications and demands for painful compromises and outright appeasement by the Labor coalition of parties, the first historical peace treaty between the most formidable Arab state and the State of Israel was signed by Menachem Begin, leader of the Likud and a loyal disciple of the founder of Revisionist Zionism, Zeev Jabotinsky.

The peace treaty did not come about with ease. During the 18 months between the day of Sadat's arrival in Jerusalem and the signing of the peace treaty, there were many agonizing moments, periods of despair and the re-occurrence of the ugly internal struggle between the Left and the Right within the Jewish Community of Israel.

The two major trouble spots concerned Palestinian independence and the return of all land (whether liberated or conquered) by Israel during the Six Day

War.

To make matters even more difficult for Israel's negotiators, the Americans were perceived to favor Sadat over Begin, demanding more "flexibility" from Israel.

In the midst of these difficult negotiations, Israel's Left returned to its perennial role of siding with the enemy, by demonstrating against the government and conducting clandestine negotiations with Egypt.

At this time Sadat discovered an opportunity to get more than he bargained for at Camp David. Consequently, he pushed the Americans to pressure Begin for more concessions, while negotiating with Israel's opposition leaders such as Shimon Peres and Yigal Allon.

In his attempt to be conciliatory without prejudicing Israel's security and its hold on sacred biblical land, Begin accepted the concept of autonomy for Palestinian Arabs living within the territory liberated by Israel during the Six Day War. On the other hand, he adamantly refused to "return to pre-1967 borders" or to recognize an independent Palestinian State.

These delicate negotiations were made more difficult by ugly and often turbulent pressures for "flexibility" by the combined forces of "Peace Now" and the Left Labor coalition headed by Shimon Peres and Itzhak Rabin.

In their book "Menachem Begin: From Freedom Fighter to Statesman," Hirschler and Eckman commented: "The Carter Administration, aware that Labor Alignment partisans in Israel, along with many Jews in the United States, had not made their peace with the change in Israel's government, began to drop hints that perhaps peace in the Middle East might be attained more readily if someone other than Begin were prime minister of Israel". [4]

The "honeymoon" was over. The Leftist press, politicians and commentators resumed their personal attacks on Begin, demanding his resignation and accusing him of expansionism and war mongering.

Of course Begin struck back at his accusers. He was bitter to find sabotage instead of support from former leaders of Israel. He ridiculed the world press for "relying on the diagnosis of Dr. Peres and Dr. Allon" (former Foreign Minister) who he said characterized him as senile.

"Did I ever refer to Golda Meir as senile when she served as prime minister at 75, or Ben-Gurion, who served until he was 80?" Begin protested. As a member of National Unity Government under Levi Eshkol, he was well aware of the Prime Minister's failing health, but he, Begin, had never said a word to anyone. [5]

Concerning charges of being an "obstacle to peace," Begin parried that he was only an obstacle to Israeli surrender on Arab terms rather than to peace.

Finally, Begin drew the attention of Israeli citizens to the fact that Labor Alignment leaders are well-versed in the art of "character assassination" by reminding them that their own former chief, Ben Gurion, had faired no better at their hands than had their arch-adversary, Jabotinsky, some 40 years ago. Throughout the 1930s they labeled Jabotinsky a fascist and now, when Ben Gurion and his Rafi comrades left Mapai, they called them "neo-fascists". [6]

Nevertheless, in spite of bitter debates in the Knesset and enormous pressures from the Carter White House, a no-confidence motion introduced by Labor was soundly rejected and all alternative policy proposals were defeated by votes of 70 to 35.

Sensing a complete political fiasco, Carter, with his thoughts fixed on his own re-election, decided to invite both Begin and Sadat to a "make it-or break it" summit at Camp David in Maryland's Catoctin Mountains. The rest is history.

****

Peace with Egypt did not come easy. But it came at a much lower price than that advocated by Israeli Left. Nevertheless, even among Begin's staunchest supporters and colleagues there was deep and bitter dissension. However, once the peace treaty was ratified by the Knesset, every one fell in line and Begin's popularity climbed to its highest level.

With Israel's southern border secured by a peace treaty with Egypt, the government of Israel was faced with a serious threat in the north. Syria refused to talk to Israel, ruling out any form of negotiations.

In the meantime Syria's dictator Hafez Assad was openly instigating and assisting Arafat's PLO build up of influence and military force in Lebanon. His interest in supporting the Palestinian terrorists was two fold: On one hand Syria was preparing an eventual subjugation of Lebanon while, on the other, it was more than happy to fight its enemy—Israel—till the last Palestinian "martyr."

PLO Chief Yassir Arafat, on the other hand, having been forcefully ejected by Jordan, was becoming increasingly dependent on Syria's support and assistance. The Soviet Union, likewise, was more than willing to supply Arafat with weapons ranging from machine guns to missiles and from explosives to armored vehicles. As a result, the military arsenal of the Palestinian radicals became large enough to sustain them over years of sabotage and combat against the State of Israel.

Besides being prodded militarily by Syria and the Soviet Union, Arafat also received undivided political and diplomatic assistance from the European Union and the Arab League, the United Nations and the "peaceniks" in Israel.

Thus terror became an acceptable tactic of Fatah and all its splinter groups such as Hamas, Hazbollah, Islamic Jihad and others. As a result Israel's northern region was being constantly subjected to bombardment, either from heavy weapons fired from the Lebanon border or from suicide attacks of armed Palestinian terrorists also finding a safe haven in Lebanon.

This situation became both frustrating and intolerable. Lebanon's government was too weak to cope with the PLO and therefore had little to say in the matter. In fact, for practical purposes Lebanon became known as "Fatah land," controlled by Arafat and his men and supported and appeased by the Arab League, the United Nations, the European Union and the Union of the Soviet Socialist Republics.

In the meantime the inhabitants of Israel's northern towns such as Kiryat Shmonah and Metullah were under constant attack by Katusha rockets as well as by suicide assassins stationed, trained and armed behind the safety of the Lebanese border.

Serious as it was, the situation on the northern borders of Israel was not the most urgent priority on the minds of the prime minister of Israel and his military command.

It was known to Israel's intelligence for some time now that Iraq, with the help of the French scientists was developing a nuclear capability.

For some time Begin was troubled by secret reports indicating that Iraq's atomic reactor at Osiraq was about to "go hot." This meant that Iraq would shortly possess the critical quantity of fissionable material.

No efforts were spared by Israel's diplomatic corps to address the danger by appealing, in vain, to both the French and the American governments to pressure Iraq to halt that work. However, once again, the world remained indifferent to this new mortal danger facing Israel. This was the time for decisive action.

After sleepless nights and weeks of thought and evaluation, Menachem Begin reached his decision to destroy the reactor. He shared these thoughts only with Defense Minister Gen. Sharon, the Chief of Staff Gen. Eytan and the officers who would be directly involved in carrying out the dangerous assignment.[7]

On June 7, 1981, the carefully planned operation was carried out. The Prime Minister was at home in Jerusalem when Chief of Staff Eytan telephoned to report: "The boys have set out." "Let us hope for the best," Begin replied and called for an urgent cabinet meeting.

No one knew the reason why they were gathered in such urgency. At five o'clock on Sunday afternoon Begin reported to his cabinet: "Welcome my friends. At this very moment our planes are approaching Baghdad and the first will be over the reactor in a very short time." The Prime Minister continued to explain that according to reliable information the reactor would become operational by July or August. By then it would be too late to destroy it, as the operation would release huge amounts of radioactive material endangering the lives of hundreds of thousands of innocent people. "No Jew, no Israeli government, would perpetrate such a deed," he concluded.[8]

By 7 p.m. the planes returned to base reporting that the reactor was completely destroyed. Some ministers wept; others laughed; some set stunned, staring into space.[9]

An international political storm broke out the very next day. Condemnations flooded from every quarter. In America, President Ronald Reagan ordered the impounding of four F-16 jets that had already been paid for by Israel. The United Nations passed a near unanimous resolution of condemnation of the State of Israel and called for "an appropriate redress for Iraq for the destruction it has suffered."

Worst of all was the almost sick reaction from Israel's Left. Labor's leader Shimon Peres criticized the action claiming that it was "designed to attract votes with the most dangerous operation in Israel's history". [10]

This storm of protests eventually subsided but it took no less than ten years for some of the accusers to admit their error and voice a humble apology.

Subsequently, resolutions were proposed in the US Congress "thanking Israel for destroying the atomic reactor." Many senators and congressmen proclaimed gratitude with tears in their eyes. One of the harshest critics of this bombing, the "Miami Herald,' apologized to Menachem Begin and put the record straight.

In Israel too, many critics from the Left drew a remorseful retreat. Abba Eban eventually described the bombing as "one of the most dramatic decisions ever taken by the government in the nuclear age."

Even Yitzhak Rabin was among the signatories of one hundred Knesset members who paid tribute to Begin "for taking courageous unilateral action against Iraq." However, Peres, Labor's nominal leader, who in 1981 addressed "a last minute appeal" against the action and criticized it severely when it was successfully completed, refused to sign this Knesset tribute. So did the Arab members of the Knesset. . . .

Now, the time was ripe to attend to the "northern threat" posed by daily attacks from Lebanon by terrorist forces of the PLO.

There was no other way to stop these attacks and to protect Israel's citizenry but to wage a military campaign with the aim of liquidating Arafat's forces of terror.

Thus, on June 6, exactly fifteen years after Levi Eshkol ordered the IDF into action in what became known as the "Six Day War", Israeli forces crossed the Lebanese border reaching the city of Nabatiya, in southern Lebanon. This was the opening shot of the so-called "Peace for Galilee" operation.

The ultimate goal of this assault was to push back Arafat's terrorists some forty kilometers beyond the Israel-Lebanon border in order to secure Israel's north from PLO's devastating, regular attacks.

Beyond expectations, Syria decided to step in on behalf of the Palestinian terrorists by sending its air force into action, as well as activating its tank corps and missiles. As a result, the Israeli command was forced to expand the campaign, move further north and engage the Syrians on ground and in the air. Within a week the Syrians lost 102 Soviet Migs, 19 ground-to-air missiles and 405 Soviet tanks. Arafat's positions were destroyed; thousands of terrorists were killed, captured and wounded and peace was finally returned to the Galilee. [11]

It is significant to note, at this time, the different reaction of the Right and the Left to relatively similar situations, namely, fateful moments experienced by the Jewish State at the hands of an enemy.

During the wars of independence, Sinai, Six Day War and the Yom Kippur War, the nationalist element as represented by the followers of Zeev Jabotinsky, came to the support of the Government and the Armed Forces of Israel without reservations.

Here, during the very first war waged by the Right Government, the "loyal" opposition turned its back on the Army and its commanders by accusing the

Government of aggression, politics and brutality. Again, the hate syndrome of "Arlozoroff Case", the "Season" and the "Altalena" returned to undermine the unity of Israel in its time of destiny and peril.

Not only did the Labor parliamentarians indulge in oral and written criticism of the war, some went as far as to attribute atrocities to Jewish soldiers while, at the same time, appealing to them to refuse combat duties and face "bravely" the resultant court martial!

The "Peace for Galilee" operation was no doubt a costly one for Israel. It sacrificed 350 lives and more than 2,000 wounded, during the course of the war. But now, victory was at hand and peace loomed on the horizon.

In reaching an agreement with the President of the US, Begin accepted a cease-fire to be followed by Arafat's and his PLO forces' departure from Lebanon. Thus by September 14, the PLO left Beirut, replaced by the US peace-keeping forces.

Immediately following this agreement, a bomb ripped through the Phalangist headquarters in Beirut, causing enormous destruction of property and killing dozens of innocent Lebanese civilians. Among the dead was the Christian president of Lebanon, Basir Gemayel.

Although Begin was determined to prevent civil war in Lebanon, it is evident that his defense minister, Ariel Sharon, was planning to use the Christian militia to take over the camps in west Beirut. In fact, he reported that there were some 2,000 Palestinian terrorists hiding inside the Sabra and Shatila camps.

The next day, facing no resistance, the Phalangists entered both camps and began a mass slaughter of all inmates.

The uproar caused by the wanton murder of at least 300 people, continued unabated for more than six months. A commission of inquiry was set up chaired by Supreme Court Justice Yitzhak Kahan. The commission's verdict included the following major points: 1) The massacre in Sabra and Shatila had been carried out by a Phalangist unit, acting on its own; 2) No Israeli was directly responsible for the events which occurred in the camp; 3) Because the IDF (Israel Defense Forces) were in control of the area, Israel bears indirect responsibilities; and 4) A recommendation that Gen. Sharon be removed from office of Defense Minister, together with a number of high ranking auxiliary officers, including the head of military intelligence and commander of Israeli forces in the north. [12]

The world saw it differently. It accused Israel of direct responsibility; even of a carefully planned conspiracy. The most outspoken critics, along with the Arab leadership and their media, were the liberal elements of the Peace Now Movement, supported by the entire Left wing of Israel's political landscape.

Perhaps the most painful and costly price Israel paid for these developments leading to the slaughter in Sabra and Shatila, was the loss of a great patriot and historic leader of his people, Menachem Begin.

No one knows which blow fell Begin—the loss of his beloved wife Aliza, who succumbed to her chronic respiratory disease during the campaign in Lebanon—or the merciless libel of the opposition which accused him of "unnecessary deaths" of Israeli soldiers as well as of a direct responsibility for the murder of Arabs by Arabs in Sabra and Shatila. No doubt both were heavy blows to a man of his stature and compassion. The fact remains—Begin could lead no more.

In spite of pleas of his colleagues and supporters, Begin resigned from office to spend the last few years of his colorful life in privacy, bordering on isolation. He became a shadow of himself, both physically and spiritually.

The leadership of Likud was now passed on to Itzhak Shamir, who automatically took over the premiership and was soon to face the prospect of new elections.

With the replacement of Begin by a relatively colorless Shamir, the political arena of Israel was about to undergo a radical change. It was more than a change in personalities, methods and manner of governance. Begin's demise opened wide the door for a political evaluation involving the very ideologies of the two major competitors—followers of Jabotinsky on one hand and the adherents of "Social Zionism", on the other.

The new generation in both camps rebelled against the old doctrines and discarded previous values. In the case of Zionism's Right wing, the move was being generated towards the Center. The Left, on the other hand embraced the "liberalism" of the New Left, aligning itself with both the European and the American trends moving in the same direction.

This evaluation began to take place within the framework of Israel's Labor several years before the ideological meltdown began to affect the Likud. In the meantime the followers of Jabotinsky and Begin were brought into an ideological freeze, with Shamir at the helm.

It was at this juncture that the new elections were held in Israel as "Shamir's cabinet fumbled its way to collapse". [13]

The elections took place in July 1984 and culminated in a virtual draw between the two major political parties. As a result neither could form a government without the other. Consequently the two parties agreed on a government of National Unity, to be headed first by Peres, then by Shamir, on the basis of a two year rotation.

Thus Peres became the Prime Minister of Israel. But it was not the Peres of old. It was an ambitious man, aching for political power. Consequently he allied himself with Yossi Beilin ("Peres' poodle"—according to Itzhak Rabin) and Yossi Sarid of Meraz. As a result of their cooperation, Peres was completely converted to the ideology of "Peace Now" Movement, advocating appeasement and surrender of significant parts of Eretz Israel, including the "old" city of Jerusalem.

Israel had thus stepped onto a new and dangerous road ahead.

The many changes within the opposing parties of the Left and the Right included much more than personalities and their *modus operandi*. These changes precipitated a sharp devaluation of the basic ideological content on one hand and an ugly appearance of morbid egotism, on the other.

However, one of Zion's most devastating ailments remained unchanged. It was the deep, often uncontrollable hate of the Left and its new Liberal element towards conservative and nationalistic Zionism. Regretfully, this hate spread further to embrace the religious orthodoxy which in turn abandoned its tolerance of the Left and sided with those devoted to the principal of indivisibility of Eretz Israel.

This hate stood to endanger the very existence of the Jewish Homeland and cause many more tears to Zion, in the process.

Notes

1. *Menachem Begin* by Hirschler and Eckman. Published by Shengold N.Y. 1979. Page 297
2. *Menachem Begin* by Hirschler and Eckman. Page 305
3. *Jerusalem Post* November 13, 1977—Israel
4. *Menachem Begin* by Hirschler and Eckman. Pages 322-323
5. *Menachem Begin* by Hirschler and Eckman. Page 328
6. *Menachem Begin* by Hirschler and Eckman. Page 328
7. *Begin: A Portrait* by H. Hurwitz. Page 159
8. *Begin: A Portrait* by H. Hurwitz. Page 161
9. *Begin: A Portrait* by H. Hurwitz. Page 161
10. *To Win or to Die* by Ned Temko. Page 256
11. *To Win or to Die* by Ned Temko. Page 282
12. *Begin: A Portrait* by H. Hurwitz. Page 206
13. *To Win or to Die* by Ned Temko. Page 292

Chapter 12
Competing for Peace

The virtual tie of the 1988 national elections created a flaky coalition government wherein the two major parties—the Labor and the Likud—worked against each other rather than in unison of purpose and aim. If anything, the competition of the two "partners" became more intense than before, bringing forth acts of scheming, sabotage and intrigue, previously non-existent in any Israeli coalition.

The first two years between 1984 and 1986 had Shimon Peres leading the government of "National Unity" with Shamir as Foreign Minister and Itzhak Rabin as Minister of Defense.

These were two politically insignificant years with no progress made either in the realm of peace or in the military content of anti-terrorist activity.

Neither was the rotation of premiership conducive to much improvement in the overall stagnation. Now that Shamir was at the helm, Peres became Minister of Foreign Affairs while Rabin maintained his position as Minister of Defense.

During this second half of the national unity government, Peres showed his true colors by negotiating agreements with the enemy without the knowledge of his own Prime Minister. This, totally unprecedented episode involved Moshe Arens, a Likud minister without portfolio, at the time.

Arens became well known not only in Israel but also in the United States of America, where he served for several years as Israel's Ambassador. A quiet, unassuming man, Arens rose in the Movement from the ranks of Jabotinsky's Youth Organization—Betar. He was an outstanding student of aeronautics in the States and became a professor at Haifa University. Soon he was invited to become head of the engineering department of the Israel Aircraft Industries, as well as its vice-president. Arens headed the Kfir airplane project which became the mainstay fighter aircraft of Israel's Air Force.

While serving Israel as its Ambassador to Washington, Arens developed excellent relationships with many senators, congressmen and some pivotal administration personalities. Among these was Secretary of State George Shultz.

In April 1987, in his capacity as Israel's Minister of Foreign Affairs, Peres traveled to London to meet with Jordan's King Hussein. During their meeting Peres negotiated and signed an agreement with the King to organize an international conference on peace in the Middle East. Realizing that this was in complete contravention to the declared policy of the Government and all its Likud ministers, Peres decided to request the U.S. Secretary of State George Shultz to come to Israel and present this Peres-Hussein agreement as a U.S. initiative. This totally unprecedented affair was scuttled successfully due to the existing relationship between Shultz and Arens.

In his book *Broken Covenant*, Arens describes this entire maneuver in one paragraph: "On his return from London, Peres reported to Shamir in general terms about the agreement he had negotiated but refused to give him the text of the agreement. At this point, Shamir, relying on the close relationship I had established with Shultz while I was Ambassador to Washington and later Defense Minister, asked me to go to Washington and dissuade Shultz from coming on the mission that Peres had engineered behind Shamir's back. It took no more than a few minutes to explain to Shultz that the Prime Minister, as well as the Likud Party, was opposed to holding an international conference on the Middle East, and that were he to come to Israel to present the Peres-Hussein agreement, he would find himself embroiled in an internal Israeli political debate. Shultz decided not to come, and Peres never forgave me". [1]

It was in this atmosphere that the two parties completed their four year term of "rotating premiership" and faced the verdict of the nation in new elections of 1988.

Once again the election failed to prove decisive. However, this time the Likud gained a very slight advantage over Labor, while Likud's potential coalition partners on the right had enough votes to help create a tiny majority in the new Knesset.

Although many Likud activists favored a narrow based coalition, which was more likely to give Likud more ministries, Shamir, Arens and others leaned in favor of a widely based coalition with the participation of Labor.

Labor, in turn, was more than anxious to join the Likud coalition for reasons of its own. During the last few years, the Histadrut and all its ailing enterprises were on the verge of bankruptcy. It was their hope that they would be in a position to salvage their crushing economic empire by remaining in the government and finding a way to funnel financial assistance to their failing domain.

This thinking was conducive to Labor's acceptance of Shamir's offer to join Likud in a Likud-led national coalition government. This too was the reasoning behind Labor's willing acceptance of the Finance Ministry, with Shimon Peres at its head.

The Ministry of Defense was left with Rabin while Shamir offered the Foreign Ministry to Moshe Arens.

It was this 1988 Government of Itzhak Shamir that, inspired by his Foreign Minister, developed Israel's first comprehensive Peace Plan. The plan was initially developed by Arens with the aid of his young assistant, Salai Merridor.

brother of Likud's prominent member of the Knesset and Minister of Justice Dan Merridor. The initiative was based on a call for a set of conferences, including 1) a conference between Israel and all Arab countries in status of war with the Jewish State; 2) a conference of all countries supplying arms to the Middle East together with the recipient countries, to discuss ways of moderating the ongoing arms race; 3) a conference of the major industrialized nations to deal with means of alleviating the conditions of the Palestinian refugees; and 4) a call for elections amongst the Palestinians in Judea, Samaria and Gaza, for representatives who would then negotiate with Israel their status and the status of the areas in which they reside. [2]

The underlying concept of the plan was to move away from multilateral international conferences towards bilateral, direct negotiations; to concentrate on improving the economic welfare of the Palestinian population; and to eliminate fundamentalism in favor of democracy with the introduction of democratic elections among all Palestinians residing in Judea, Samaria and Gaza.

However, there were no takers to the plan and it was immediately confronted with opposition not only from the Arabs but also by the administration of George H. W. Bush, as orchestrated by its Secretary of State, James Baker.

But the most damning factor turned out to be the underhanded activities of Israel's Left, which at the time was part of the Government, supposedly sharing its goals as well as its responsibilities.

In the meantime, Shamir was preparing his visit to Washington, prior to which he called a meeting of Rabin, Peres and Arens to discuss the presentation of the Israeli peace plan to President Bush. At the meeting, (according to Arens) "Rabin objected to the clause dealing with arms control while Peres kept his own counsel." [3]

Nevertheless, the meetings in Washington went smoothly and President Bush seemed to respond favorably to Shamir's presentation.

The reaction of the Arab world was totally negative, however. This included Egypt's President Hosni Mubarak, who echoed the PLO objection to elections in favor of allowing Egypt and the United States to select the Palestinian representatives.

In his attempt to solicit help for rehabilitation of the Palestinian refugees, Arens met with ambassadors of the United States, Japan, Germany, France, Italy, the United Kingdom and Canada, to present them with a plan for their physical and economic assistance. In *Broken Covenant* Arens recalled: "When I asked them to transmit these proposals to their respective governments, I drew a complete blank. Governments that were busy criticizing Israel were evidently not prepared to make an effort to alleviate the human tragedy of the Palestinian refugees". [4]

Israel's peace initiative was further sabotaged by open hints from the Labor Party, claiming that Peres was preparing a peace plan of his own. In subsequent meetings between Shamir, Arens, Bush and Baker, it became evident that both Peres and Rabin were meeting with the Egyptians and discussing a variety of nuances to Israeli official peace initiative. All this, without the knowledge of either Shamir or Arens. Baker was very much a part of this political intrigue which seemed to favor PLO participation in the Peace Conference and an approval of a "land for peace" initiative which was known to mean a return to the pre-1967 borders.

Slowly and painfully the parties were moving onwards to a very insignificant compromise. Ignoring Israel's objections, it was decided to organize a conference of all concerned parties—Syria, Lebanon, Jordan, Egypt and representatives of the Palestinians residing in "occupied territories" (meaning Gaza, Samaria and Judea). But even at this juncture Israel was afflicted by the internal struggle waged by the Labor ministers. Of course it was not the first time that the Left tried to subvert a government in which they served; but it was certainly the first time that any U.S. Administration had intervened in Israel's internal affairs to further a policy of its own. This was done by clandestine and secret meetings conducted between Rabin and Baker. To add to this abnormal state of affairs, Egypt's Mubarak, sensing that more concessions could be expected from Israel's Labor, continued to negotiate and even reach agreements directly with Rabin and Peres, keeping both Shamir and Arens at bay.

In spite of all the intrigue and ill-will, the parties agreed to come together in Madrid for an introductory Peace Conference, which was to lead to further, detailed negotiations to be held directly between Israel and the Arab states surrounding it.

It should be noted, however, that the parties involved in this Madrid Conference came there with totally irreconcilable ideas. They were brought together by virtue of American promises and diplomatic machinations. The Palestinians were assured of U.S. Government's support for their eventual statehood, while the Israelis were equally assuaged by American agreement to exclude the PLO from the negotiating process, accepting instead a joint Jordanian-Palestinian delegation.

Thus the Israelis came to Madrid hoping to negotiate with the Palestinian-Jordanian delegation a reaffirmation of the Camp David autonomy agreement, which was to last for five years to be followed by a permanent arrangement. The Palestinians, on the other hand, arrived determined to negotiate Israel's withdrawal to the pre-1967 borders and the establishment of an independent Palestinian State.

The Americans hoped to achieve a miracle by creating a "momentum for peace" or, failing this, to help Labor win the next elections in Israel, to smooth the way for Israel's eventual "flexibility".

The negotiations in Madrid were followed with bilateral meetings in Madrid and in Washington. They turned out to be nothing but an exercise in futility.

In the meantime, elections in Israel gave Rabin an opportunity to form the next Government. With Likud out of the picture, Rabin chose to include Shas (the religious party composed of immigrants from lands of the Middle East) as well as Yossi Sarid's Meraz Party of the extreme Liberal-Left, in his new government.

While Rabin and his ministers were struggling to move the peace negotiations (now in Washington) from the dead end, reticent and deceptive arrangements were being made by Peres, Beilin and friends, under the umbrella of the Norwegian Foreign Minister Johan Jorgen Host. "Israelis were there" writes a leading Mid-East observer and commentator, Yigal Carmon, in his article: "The Story Behind the Handshake", "for one of the most momentous diplomatic moves in the history of the country without having consulted a single military authority, a single intelligence officer, or a single expert on Arab affairs." [5]

In fact, Yitzhak Rabin, the prime minister himself, was informed of the Oslo agreements only when they were ready and awaiting his signature.

Unexpectedly, a major problem developed. This was the result of another about face by the PLO representatives at Oslo, who originally accepted having the agreements endorsed and signed in Washington by representatives of the Jordanian-Palestinian delegation then conducting the official meetings with Rabin's men. It was essential to do so due to the basic premise of Rabin's (and previously, Shamir's) government not to recognize Arafat or the PLO and to deal only with representatives from Jordan and the "territories" (e.g. Gaza, Judea and Samaria).

However, when an agreement was reached in Oslo, Arafat reneged on the commitment and insisted that he and Rabin sign the Oslo document on behalf of the PLO and Israel, respectively.

By now, Rabin was caught in a web from which he would not successfully disengage. If he would not agree to sign with Arafat, he would have to return to first base and admit failure after having promised the electorate that he was the only one capable of reaching an agreement with the Palestinians. Thus, Rabin relented and agreed to come to Washington for the infamous handshake.

The Oslo agreement included Israel's acceptance of the "land for peace" principle, indicating its acknowledgment of the eventual establishment of a Palestinian State in Gaza, Judea and Samaria. The Palestinians, on the other hand, committed themselves to recognizing the State of Israel, rejecting the use of force and establishing a "council" on the principal of free and democratic elections.

Thus Arafat was brought back to Ramallah, the PLO was recognized as the representative body of the Palestinian Arabs and Israel was committed to recognize the eventual establishment of an independent Palestinian State. Two other significant matters were left for further negotiations. These concerned the return of Palestinian refugees to their abandoned homes in the State of Israel and the establishment of a Palestinian capital in East Jerusalem. Furthermore, the PLO agreed to amend its Covenant, eliminating the clause affirming its aim to be the destruction of Israel.

On the morrow of the White House handshake the PLO reneged on all its commitments. It did not amend its Covenant. It insisted on immediate moves towards sovereignty in violation of its agreement to defer such sovereignty for five years. It did not crack down on Hamas and other extremist organizations, allowing terror to continue unabated.

On the contrary, violence increased and included the participation of Fatah—the military branch of the PLO.

On September 13, 1993, the very day the DOP (Declaration of Principals) was signed in Washington; Jordanian television aired a speech by Arafat, which explained his peace policy to his own people, in Arabic. He said: "Brothers, beloved ones; Palestine is only a stone throw away for a small Palestinian boy or girl. It is the Palestinian State that lives deep in our heart. Its flag will fly over the walls of Jerusalem, the churches of Jerusalem and the mosques of Jerusalem. They see the day, indeed as a far off event, but we see it quite near and we indeed are truthful." [6]

In the light of all of the aforesaid, it was stunning to observe Israeli officials soliciting European and American financial support for the PLO, gesturing "good will" by releasing hundreds of arrested Palestinian Arab terrorists, and muting Israel's outrage over continuing violence against its citizens. And all this was being perpetrated by a government which was hanging on with a majority of a few Knesset votes, including those of five Arab members not too keen on Israel's survival.

Constant demands by the opposition to "go to the people" in a plebiscite which should approve or reject the giving away of land and tolerating continued violence remained unanswered. The population was becoming less tolerant of appeasement and more outspoken on behalf of action. Rabin's Government was being criticized severely and often savagely.

It was in the midst of this environment that a lone assassin, Yigal Amir, carried a revolver to a Labor rally at Tel Aviv's Kings of Israel Square (presently renamed—The Rabin Square). When Rabin descended from the platform and kneeled to enter into his car, Yigal pressed the trigger and shot him dead.

Even before Rabin took his last breath, the Left began to point fingers at the Likud and its newly elected young leader, Benjamin Netanyahu. The ugly ghosts of the Arlozoroff Case reappeared mirroring the most painful days in the relatively short history of the Zionist Movement.

The thorough inquiry into the murder showed clearly and irrevocably that Amir had no accomplices and was acting on his own. This did not stop the wild accusations, based on heated statements issued during political demonstrations, in articles and from the rostrum of the Knesset.

Of course, it was easy to find provocation. Some prominent rabbis spoke strongly against abandonment of portions of the Holy Land. Demonstrations against surrender of the new settlements were also portrayed as treason. There was no end to daily protests against the chain of concessions offered the PLO in return for empty promises and unrelenting acts of terror and sabotage. These protests were accompanied by angry denunciations and threats.

Yigal Amir may have well been influenced by one or all of these factors. His act was a tragedy for Israel as a whole. But it was the abandonment of pure

Zionism that was the prime motif that triggered the deed. Amir was a religious rightist, acting completely on his own impulse and prompted by belief in the historic necessity of his action. Ironically, the Likud had never been part of Yigal's political background. Nevertheless, according to a well known Jewish journalist, Hillel Halkin, "one can point to the exact historical moment when the center dropped out of Israeli politics leaving an overwhelmingly secular Left and a heavily religious Right facing each other across a discourseless chasm. But although this happened with the signing of the Oslo Agreement, culturally it was a long while in the making." [7]

By the time of this tragedy, the ideological evolution in Zionism was well on its way. To the two major components, the Left and the Right, a third had been added after the Six Day war: The Religious Right—composed of young elements of orthodoxy bent on salvaging the threatened liberated areas of Eretz Israel. The bulk of these youngsters came from "Agudat Israel" and the National Religious Party. Most of them were brought up in the ranks of their youth movements which united under the name of "Gush Emunim" (the Union of the Faithful). It is this element that spearheaded the pioneering effort of the new settlements in Judea and Samaria. They were joined by others from the nationalistic right as well as from new olim (immigrants) from American orthodoxy. Together they became the outspoken leaders of the movement to resist surrender of portions of Eretz Israel in general and abandonment of the newly established settlements, in particular.

The traditional Left of the Zionist Movement previously embodied in the major Labor Party of Mapai, had now split wide open into a variety of factions including the new Liberal Left, which became the carbon copy of the American New Liberals—be they Jews or Gentiles.

Although the declared framework for the New Liberal Leftists was Sarid's Meraz Party, many Labor followers of these internationalists and appeasers, for reasons of loyalty and sentiment, remained in the ranks of Labor. Through the untiring efforts of Yossi Beilin, both Peres and eventually Rabin became converts to this new trend on the Israeli political scene.

What happened to Jabotinsky's followers on the Right is still a mystery to many. But not to all.

During Jabotinsky's days the mainstay of Revisionism was the Youth Movement Betar. It was in Betar that the social philosophy and political ideology were developed. It was from the leading Betarim that the Hebrew underground was established and sustained. And it was from the ranks of the youth movement that future leadership of the Revisionist Movement and the Herut Party flourished. Jabotinsky himself put much effort in educating the Betar youths embracing them with his love and devotion.

Gradually, following the establishment of the State, Menachem Begin, a former leader of the Polish Betar himself, began to ignore the future prospects of the Youth Organization, leaving it to the care of others less involved in the political welfare of the Herut Movement.

As a result, from the late 1960s, Betar ceased to exist as a nucleus for its political parent—the "Herut." On the contrary, young members of Betar, often influenced by the liberal trend of the "modern" environment in Israel, drew away from Jabotinsky's political ideology as well as his social philosophy.

Also, when Herut opened its gates to all comers, first as "Gahal" and later as "Likud," it gradually shredded much of Jabotinsky's principles of selfless idealistic monism; absorbing instead the modern "culture" of individual and collective opportunism.

Thus, by the time of Rabin's assassination on November 4, 1995, Israel was experiencing the throes of its cultural and political evolution. All parties affiliated with Herzl's Zionist Congress have undergone changes beyond recognition and to many Israelis and Jews of the Diaspora, the very goals of Zionism became hazy and questionable.

It was in such an atmosphere that Israel faced its new national elections of 1996. The population was exhausted from constant sacrifices, casualties and fruitless negotiations with enemies bent on its total destruction.

As a result, the young, inspiring leader of the "Likud," Benjamin Netanyahu overwhelmingly won the confidence of the People in the first direct elections for the Prime Minister in the State of Israel. Together with their coalition partners, the Likud had no problem to garnering enough seats in the Knesset to give Netanyahu a comfortable majority to govern.

Although Netanyahu defeated Peres from the Labor Party quite significantly, he was either unable or unwilling to move too abruptly away from the promises made to and agreements reached with the PLO. This was his major error. His attitude was perceived as weakness. His other mistake was in the arrogant attitude he displayed towards his own comrades—the Herut faithful such as Arens, Merridor, Landau, Olmert and others. He chose to surround himself with his cheering squad rather than with the deserving veterans of the Party. As a result, he lost the support of many.

During the three years as Prime Minister, Netanyahu succeeded in improving the economy but failed to unite his own Party which seemed to be losing its ideological mandate as well as its political compass.

In the meantime, Ehud Barak completed his excellent service as head of the Armed Forces of Israel and submitted his candidacy for premiership, under the banner of Peres' Labor Party. In view of his popularity as a courageous warrior, Barak was immediately given preference over Peres within Labor. Following this internal victory, he had no problem winning the national elections of 1999 to become the second prime minister to be elected directly by the People.

Tragically instead of turning his back on appeasement (as was expected of him by many) Barak decided to melt his sword into a plowshare and embraced both Sarid and Beilin, inviting them to join his Cabinet. Subsequently it was this cabinet that adopted a new philosophy of "peace at any price. . . ."

And, in fact, this became the new direction of the newly elected Liberal Left Government of Israel. As a result, more blood and more tears were yet to be shed.

Notes

1. *Broken Covenant* by Moshe Arens. Published by Simon and Schuster, New York 1995. Page 23
2. *Broken Covenant* by Moshe Arens. Page 44
3. *Broken Covenant* by Moshe Arens. Pages 60-61
4. *Broken Covenant* by Moshe Arens. Pages 62
5. *The Mideast Peace Process* by Yigal Carmon in a book edited by Kozochoy. Published by Encounter Books. San Francisco. Page 17
6. *The Mideast Peace Process* by Yigal Carmon in a book edited by Kozochoy. Published by Encounter Books. San Francisco. Pages 26-27
7. *The Rabin Assassination: A Reckoning*, Article written by Hillel Halkin in *The Commentary Journal*, Jan. 1996

Chapter 13
Zionism on Brink of Disaster

The devastation of Zionism did not begin with Barak, Sarid, Beilin or the "Peace Now" Movement. It developed slowly, leaning on the growth and development of new Liberalism and internationalism, which had penetrated the political scene of America and began to run amuck in most of modern Europe.

Although Peres, and later Rabin, adopted the New Left's concept of self-denigration and began to promote "universalism," the ideological decay of Zionism began to appear long before "Peace Now" became an acceptable fraction of the Zionist mode.

The Left's denial of monistic Zionism from the first days of Herzlian efforts on behalf of Jewish statehood and its introduction of monopolistic tendencies to control the Movement and the resultant internal strife, were the seeds from which further rejections of unifying nationalism sprouted.

However, there exists an enormous distance between Ben Gurion's attempt at creating a nation entrenched in its history and heritage and the efforts of the New Liberal Left, to destroy it. And, although the better known promoters of this destructive tendency to revise Jewish history, redefine Zionism and erase the proud heritage of the People of Israel, are Ehudith Aloni, Yossi Sarid, Yossi Beilin and their followers, the actual architects are the Israeli academics who have been "overseeing the attenuation of the Zionist perspective in Israeli education since the early 1990s. It is a process whose implications for Barak's government—and for all of Israeli society—we are only beginning to understand."[1]

When Ben Gurion and his education minister, Benzion Dinur, designed the curriculum for high school history study, it was meant to be a patriotic, national endeavor to teach the young generation of Israelis the Jewish history depicting a unique people who, after centuries of persecution—culminating with the horrors of the Holocaust—have returned to their land to build a Jewish State as a just conclusion of this millennial struggle.

The Israeli school system was created by the State Education Law which Dinur introduced to the Knesset in 1953. Its main concern was that Israel's schools include in the curriculum: "the values of Jewish culture," "love of the homeland," and "loyalty to the Jewish State." To achieve this, the prescribed studies included the Bible, Jewish history, Talmud and Jewish thought, as well as courses on the "motherland," studies of Israeli geography, natural history and archeology. All this for the purpose of "rooting the children in the Land of Israel". [2]

Since then, much of Israel's academia fell under the influence of the extreme left wing of the Labor Movement. Gradually, individuals from this wing were immersed into the currents of the New Liberalism, in concert with their colleagues in Europe and the United States of America.

This new "culture" of universalism punctuated Israeli literature, theatre, journalism and education. It was only logical that it would affect seriously and detrimentally the curriculum in Israeli schools and universities.

The curriculum committees were dominated by proponents of the new trend. One of its prime movers was Prof. Israel Bartal of the Jewish history department at Hebrew University. Another was Prof. Michael Heyd, who came to chair an Education Ministry committee responsible for revising the high school history curriculum.

It was Prof. Heyd who commented on the necessity for revision thus: "There is no longer one accepted historic truth. The old history books, which in earlier years presented the Zionist narrative as an undisputed historical fact, do not fit in with the (present) historical and political discourse after the myths have been smashed. You can't ignore Israel's transformation into a multicultural society." [3]

Another prominent member of the committee for revising the high school and university curriculum was a history professor of the Hebrew University—Prof. Moshe Zimmerman. His views of "universal history" as a replacement for the concept of unique Jewish nationality, has also been incorporated into the history curriculum. It first emerged in the summer of 2000, when the *New York Times* broke the story that in the wake of the peace process, text books approved by the Education Ministry (under Yossi Sarid) "contained the information that some of the Arab population of Palestine was expelled by Jewish forces during 1948 War of Independence and that the Jews enjoyed numerical superiority over the Arabs during that war." [4]

Similar and bolder revisions appear today in schools dealing with archeology as well as the study of citizenship.

The efforts to create a "universal" curriculum have succeeded beyond imagination. But the most painful example is the altered presentation of Jerusalem's 1967 unification. This phase is best articulated in Yoram Hazoni's well-read article: "Who Removed Zionism from Israel's Text Books?" which appeared in *The New Republic*, on April 17 and 24, in 2000. Hazoni wrote: "In the old books, the struggle over Jerusalem is told the way most people remember it: as the result of a war with Jordan that Israel did not want but that, due to Jordan's insistence on entering the war, ended with some of the most heroic battles of Israeli history and with the return of the Jews to the Temple Mount. The old Education Ministry textbook described it thus:

'With the outbreak of fighting on the Egyptian front, the Jordanians began bombarding Jerusalem. Israel warned King Hussein not to join the war, but he ignored the warning . . . so that fighting erupted on this front as well . . . On the night between June 5 and 6, forces from the paratroops broke through Jordanian defenses in north Jerusalem in brutal battles on Ammunition Hill and in the area of the Rockefeller museum, and on the morning of June 7 they stormed through the Lion's Gate into the Old City.'

"The new books have none of this—no Israeli pleas for Jordan to stay out of the war, no heroic battles, no Western Wall. Instead, there is only this:

'Later the Jordanians and the Syrians joined the war. . . . Israel captured expansive territories...including East Jerusalem from the Jordanians. . . . After the war, the Israeli government decided to annex East Jerusalem, including the Old City.'

Hazoni concludes his important article with these thoughts: "Until now, Israelis have paid little attention to the school-book revolution. The Golan Heights, the PLO, and related topics remain virtually the entire policy agenda of both the Labor and the Likud parties. But the old Zionist curriculum wasn't just any old piece of policy. As Ben-Gurion understood, the cultural common ground it represented held the disparate groups within Israeli Jewry together. It was an important part of what makes Israeli Jews a single people." *

No doubt these painful, if not treasonable, revisions played havoc with Zionism as a whole, as well as with the national spirit of idealism and pride.

To briefly summarize the scope of the atrocities of the revised educational curriculum, it may suffice to mention that while seven books in the old curriculum were devoted to the Holocaust and the Warsaw Ghetto uprising, the new text does not even mention the existence of such horrors on one hand and such acts of supreme heroism—on the other.

It was onto this field of anti-Zionist revisionism that premier Barak came to sow his seeds of appeasement, bordering on total abandonment of the Zionist cause.

In spite of this background, the Israelis voted for Barak only because of his valorous military service and his personal courage and determination. His teaming up with the religious parties and Natan Sharansky's nationalistic "Israel B' Aliya" Party of Russian immigrants, was therefore not surprising. What became astonishing however, was his eventual leaning towards the anti-Zionist ideology of the "universalists" such as Sarid and Beilin.

The honeymoon between the Zionist parties in the government and Barak did not last long. The split came about when Barak's Education Minister Yossi Sarid decided to include a number of poems by Mahmoud Darwish (an outspoken anti-Semite and an opponent of the 1993 Oslo accords) in Israel's high school literature curriculum. One of these poems read: "Don't pass among us like flying insects. / The time has come for you to leave. / Live where you will but don't live amongst us. / The time has come for you to leave."

Objecting to this latest assault on the existing curriculum, both the Shas Party and the National Religious Party, together with Sharansky, decided to leave the Government, leaving Barak and Meratz, with the support of 7 Arab votes, to continue leading the nation into catastrophic negotiations under the tutelage of President William Clinton.

The fact that this minority government continued to hold vital, even existence-threatening, negotiations only underlines its arrogance. The fact that this government's voting majority came from the seven Arab members of the Knesset underlines its moral vulgarity. Be it as it may, Barak, Clinton and Arafat were locked into negotiations that were to determine the very question of Israel's future. Clearly 50% of Israel's Jewish population was against the trend these negotiations were taking and supported the opposition's demand for a national referendum.

Across the ocean, in America, the Zionists continued to support the Left Government of Barak. Any opposition to its policy of total appeasement was too mute to be evident. The reasons were obvious.

American Jewry in its majority has been known to support Labor in Israel and the Democratic Party in America. In addition, Jews of America were among the foremost proponents of the New Liberal Left. They were in the forefront of the anti-Vietnam Movement marching in protest on the streets of all major cities in the United States. And they were the loudest cheer-leaders of the Rabin-Arafat hand-shake and Clinton-Barak's proposals to give Arafat Gaza, Judea, Samaria and Eastern Jerusalem, for a promise of "peace".

In the United States, Jewish opposition to the Israel Government's readiness to surrender the settlements, Jerusalem and the Golan Hights was restricted to the few faithful among the old followers of Jabotinsky, augmented by an ever increasing number of Orthodox Jews. This, no doubt, was part of a growing Jewish disenchantment with America's Liberal Left, a disenchantment which is increasing in proportion with the growth of the Jewish Orthodoxy.

In his article "The Election and the Jewish Vote", Jay Lefkowitz** writes: "As far as the Republican party is concerned, Orthodox Jews clearly hold the greatest potential. Even though they make up only a tenth of the Jewish Community, they are growing much faster than the secular branches, which are shrinking, due to assimilation, inter-marriage, and lower birth rates. As Orthodox Jewry increases in numbers, we may conceivably see a softening of the once unwavering commitment of Jewish voters to an impermeable wall of separation between church and state and a greater receptivity to the "values" positions associated with the GOP".

Much the same could be said regarding the attitude of American Jewry to Israel's socialists of old—the Left Liberals of today—who embrace internationalism and appeasement and who are ready to have Israel give up every one of the new settlements in order to receive applause from the anti-Semites of Europe and the Left-Liberals of America.

It was, therefore, this combination of anti-Zionist forces that presented themselves as an "appropriate" background from which both Clinton and Barak could engage, unobtrusively, in negotiations with Ararat, that led to the most extravagant concessions any previous American President dared to propose and any previous Israeli Prime Minister dare to accept.

These sentiments, drawing their strength and logic from a demoralized society of the "Peace Now" advocates and the battle-fatigued majority of Israelis, enabled Barak and Clinton to pursue their plan of "total appeasement".

Daniel Pipes[†] wrote in his article "Israel's Moment of Truth": "Israelis are tired of the moral opprobrium their country has long suffered at the UN, in Western academic circles, and in editorial boardrooms. According to a survey of the Jaffe Center at Tel Aviv University, fully two-thirds of Israelis now agree with the following dubious assertions that most Palestinians want peace; that signing agreements will end the Arab-Israeli conflict; and that if forced to choose between negotiations and increased military strength, Israel should opt for the former".[5]

This general atmosphere in Israel blended well with the new educational curriculum in schools and universities, wherein patriotism was eliminated and universalism/internationalism promoted.

It also blended well with the Liberal-Left philosophy of the majority within the Jewish Community of America. Therefore, the first stages of the Clinton-Barak-Arafat negotiations were met with loud approval and enthusiastic encouragement.

The stage was set now for Clinton and Barak to place before Arafat Israel's agreement—with full backing of the US Government—to return 97% of the liberated areas of Gaza, Judea and Samaria, allow the establishment of a Palestinian State with its capital in East Jerusalem, abandonment of all settlements in Gaza, Judea and Samaria, and a return of an unspecified (to be agreed on) number of Palestinian "refugees".

Of course, this suicidal proposal was to lean on several commitments to be made by the PLO. These were not spelled out but were understood to include: Recognition of the State of Israel, armament moderation, and other instruments for peaceful co-existence. It was at this final stage in negotiations that the entire peace process suddenly collapsed.

By now, Ararat decided that he has gone too far in the direction of "peace". He believed that by accepting Clinton-Barak concessions, he may be forced into a peace treaty which will undermine his plan for Israel's "elimination in stages." Therefore, he decided to back-pedal on the so-called negotiation for peace by demanding the "return of all refugees" clause. When this was rejected, he initiated his Intifada No 2.

There was a hidden blessing in this development, dangerous as it was. As a result, many of the "Peace Now" philosophers have accepted the fact that the PLO and the vast majority of the Palestinians do not want peace with Israel. Instead, they seek Israel's liquidation. Likewise, the honest element in the Western World began to see the true aims of the Palestinian leadership.

Most significantly, polls taken in Israel after Arafat's declaration of the new Intifada indicated that if (as promised) Barak would have submitted his "concessions" to a national plebiscite; they would have been rejected by an absolute majority of Israelis. Only in this case, rightly or wrongly, Israel would have stood condemned by history.

At this time a totally new dimension was added to the Middle East equation. The United States proper was physically attacked by Arab terrorists. Fortunately, this vile act of 9/11 took place soon after George W. Bush became the new President of the United States of America.

The new President and his Cabinet realized immediately that America is now at war with Moslem terrorism, on a world wide basis. Simultaneously, ignoring the vain attempts of the State Department to pursue its perennial pro-Arab policy, the Bush Administration openly sided with Israel's newly elected Prime Minister Ariel Sharon's strategy of confrontation with Palestinian terror. This was a significant change in official US policy, which brought Israel and America that much closer together.

Most importantly, these events helped to bring Israel back from the brink of disaster and to rescue Zionism from a total collapse. The question remained, however: For how long?

Notes

* Yoram Hazoni is president of the Shalem Center in Jerusalem. His *book The Jewish State: The Struggle of Israel's Soul* was published by New Republic/Basic Books in May 2000.

** Jay Lefkowitz served on the White House staff of President George W. Bush. He wrote, in March 2001, an article in commentary: *Does the Jewish vote count?*

† Daniel Pipes is the director of the Middle East Forum and author of *Conspiracy; How the Paranoid Style Flourishes and Where it Comes From*.

1. *Who Removed Zionism from Israel's Textbooks?* Article by Yoram Hazoni, president of Shalem Center in Jerusalem. Printed in the New Republic, on April 17, 2000.
2. *Who Removed Zionism from Israel's Textbooks?* Article by Yoram Hazoni, president of Shalem Center in Jerusalem. Printed in the New Republic, on April 17, 2000.
3. *Who Removed Zionism from Israel's Textbooks?* Article by Yoram Hazoni, president of Shalem Center in Jerusalem. Printed in the New Republic, on April 17, 2000.
4. *Who Removed Zionism from Israel's Textbooks?* Article by Yoram Hazoni, president of Shalem Center in Jerusalem. Printed in the New Republic, on April 17, 2000.
5. *Israel's Moment of Truth* by Daniel Pipes. Printed in *Contemporary* in 2000.

Chapter 14
The Dangers of Today

General Sharon became Prime Minister of Israel at a time when the Zionist evolution reached its peak. The major effects of the changes were influenced by events such as the collapse of the Soviet Union and the Eastern Bloc, the revival of European anti-Semitism, and the growth of New Liberalism in the United States of America.

As a result, the leftists of the Western world rushed to the ideological flag poles of self-consciousness and pulled down the red flags, to replace them with the banners of "Liberalism" of their own interpretation. However, the mix of the two opposing political philosophies condemned Marxism to the trash bin of history while, at the same time, it subjected true liberalism of old to the modern concept of internationalism. Thus, the leftists of today became the weavers of a new flag—a standard of radical liberalism.

Specifically, Europe, under the leadership of France and Germany, abandoned its program of post-World War II moral rehabilitation. Having opened its doors to hundreds of thousands of Arab immigrants, Western Europe abruptly turned its back not only on Israel, the creation of which they supported during the post-Hitler period, but also on the United States of America, whose sons liberated their lands from servitude under the Nazis and whose Marshal Plan helped them to overcome famine, depression and economic ruin.

Israel's Left was similarly affected. Suddenly, the May Day parades and the red flags of the Histadrut (Labor Movement's Trade Union) lost their significance, along with slogans such as: "Socialism—today!" and "Laborers of the World—Unite!" Instead, the Left parties combined under a new name: The Labor Party of Israel. That too did not last long. For the benefit of new elections the combined party again changed its name to: "One Israel". By now the Zionists and the anti-Zionists of the Labor Movement split into Labor and Meraz, respectively. However, both were influenced by the New Liberal philosophy of internationalism and appeasement.

Within Israel's Right, there was a significant move to the extreme, on one hand and towards the "middle" on the other. Parties sprang up advocating forced removal of the Arabs from Eretz Israel (Kach of the late Rabbi Kahane).

"Raful's" extremists, demanded forceful subjugation of the Arab population of Eretz Israel. The Likud, which in itself was an ideological coalition between the nationalistic, right-leaning Herut and the centrists of the former "Liberal" (General Zionist) Party of Israel, moved to the center.

Perhaps the most significant change occurred within the orthodoxy. Its major components were the Agudat Israel and the National Religious Party of Israel. Although they were members in most governments throughout Israel's existence, they have moved decidedly to the Right, after Menachem Begin's revolutionary victory at the polls in 1977.

Since then, the young members of the orthodoxy combined under the framework of "Gush Emunim" to become the major force in Likud's program of establishing settlements in order to add a physical dimension to their claim on the Land of Israel. Joining in these efforts were thousands of young men and women from both the Left and the Right Zionist youth. Indeed, the Left Labor Party of Israel was itself promoting such settlements until the "New Liberal" influence of Sarid and Beilin began to dominate the Party, with the help of its veteran leader Shimon Peres.

By the time Sharon took over as the new Prime Minister of Israel, the Zionist political map had been changed significantly. There now remained four prominent forces in play: The Likud on the Right of Center, the settlers on the extreme Right, the Zionist Labor on the Left of Center and the Left extremists of Meraz with the support of their allies remaining within the framework of Labor, prompted by sentiment and habit.

At the same time, Zionists in America, who perennially supported Israel's Left and voted for the U.S. Democratic Party, also shifted with the trend. They were subjected to the winds of the New Liberals of America who, at large, succeeded in hijacking the majority in the Democratic Party.

This is not to say that the majority of Jews, who did not vote for George W. Bush, did not support the State of Israel. Not really. No doubt, they mistakenly continued to fear Republican conservatism for their ancient sin of Christian fundamentalism, which expressed itself in occasional anti-Semitism. The fact that this feature of American Christian Community has died after Hitler and was permanently buried after Patrick Buchanan, escapes many elderly Jews, still living in the days of Roosevelt's Liberalism and socialistic reforms.

The facts speak for themselves. In today's America, Christianity as a whole and evangelism in particular, are Israel's best friends and ardent supporters.

Jay Lefkowitz, in his book *Does the Jewish Vote Count?* describes the situation with logic and insight. He writes that only 20% of Jews voting for Bush said his relationship to Israel was the primary reason for their choice, while 55% cited his efforts against Islamic terrorism. "What this suggests", he explains, "is that, for a significant number of American Jews, concern over Israel's security has merged with terrorism and anti-Semitism into a single broad issue. Whereas the threat of anti-Semitism was once almost universally perceived by American Jews as stemming from the Right, and in particular from conservative Christianity, now a portion of the community has come to understand both contemporary anti-Semitism and the threat of physical violence against Jews and Israel as deriving from a very different source—not just Islamism but also the international Left and its supporters in the Liberal media." [1]

It was only logical to expect that under such circumstances, Sharon and Bush were to create an unprecedented alliance between Israel and the United States. As a result, it was also natural that the vast majority of Israelis have come to support and to applaud President George W. Bush, even in greater numbers than their support of their own Prime Minister.

This unprecedented alliance gave Israel the opportunity to strike at Palestinian terror with full force. Although opposed by the Liberal Left, Ariel Sharon successfully directed Israeli intelligence and it's Defense Forces into combat to destroy the leadership and the infrastructure of the combined Palestinian terror movement. Likewise, together with President Bush, Sharon succeeded in isolating Yassir Arafat, both politically and physically until his final demise in the French hospital on the outskirts of Paris.

While Israel was destroying the brain trust and the physical "nest" of Palestinian terror, President Bush waged war on international Moslem fundamentalism by liberating both Afghanistan and Iraq.

These then were the major areas of success of the two allies. However, there were also some major misconceptions.

One political blunder was Bush's enthusiastic promotion of the "Road Map". The "Road Map" has been authored by the so-called "Quartet": The US, the EU, the UN and Russia. It is only logical to assume that the author's aim to supervise its implementation. In the meantime, Israel has accepted this concept "in principle" with some reservations. This was a grave error which may yet cost the cause of Zionism set backs and frustrations, and the cause of Zion—(Israel) more agony and tears. . . .

Israel should have rejected the "Road Map" not only because of its content but rather because of its authors. The European Union has been a constant mouthpiece for all Arab regimes. Its loudest voices came from Germany and France—both known for their renewed anti-Semitism during the last decade. The Russians have been the major arms suppliers of every Arab State and terrorist organization. The United Nations, this international joke in the eyes of sober political scientists, passed hundreds of anti-Israel resolutions but failed to condemn any Arab aggression and terror against the State of Israel, even once.

This then, is the composition of the infamous "Quartet".   In it, America would be out-balanced, out-talked and out-voted on each and every turn.

Another major error of Prime Minister Sharon—an error enthusiastically supported by President Bush—is a decision to vacate all settlements in Gaza and four in Northern Samaria, on the basis of "strategic necessity". Sharon decided to do so unilaterally, with or without a previous agreement with the Palestinian leadership.

This decision is violently challenged by a part of the Likud membership and by all members of the settlement movement.

Some believed that Sharon's major error was to have gone through with this plan and to reject the proposal for a plebiscite. In refusing the people the right to determine, he acted no different from his early predecessor Itzhak Rabin, who also refused the demand of the opposition to go to a plebiscite on his Oslo concessions.

It may well be that Sharon's reticent plan was to encourage such threats as were often heard from the settlers as well as an appearance of an impending catastrophe. He may have wished to demonstrate to the world at large the impossibility of surrendering any additional territory to the Palestinians. It is indeed conceivable that in spite of his readiness to give up Gaza and the smaller four settlements on the "West Bank", Mr. Sharon will be calling a halt to any further withdrawals.

Whether this indeed is his plan or not does not excuse him for ignoring the will of his electorate. No doubt it was his moral duty to accept the call for a plebiscite and to tailor his future plans accordingly. Instead, he invited the Labor opposition to join him in a coalition which is to preside over a forceful eviction of Jews from their homes and to present this land to the Palestinians, for nothing in return.

On the other hand, it must be noted that the actual process of withdrawal for Gaza was less complicated than anticipated. This goes to credit the sensitivities, patriotism and the spirit of fraternity of both the military and the settlers themselves. Regretfully, this did not relieve the Sharon Administration from renewed pressure by the American President and the newly elected President of the PLO, to demand from Israel, continued dismantling of other settlements in both Judea and Samaria.

Certainly, there are many in Israel, and elsewhere, who consider this move out of Gaza nothing short of a brilliant strategic maneuver. There are others who see it as a serious political blunder.

Of course, there are but a few citizens in Israel better equipped to determine the right military moves than the capable and talented Gen. Sharon. However, the pull-out from Gaza was not made in the form of a strategic (military) withdrawal, often necessitated in war. Rather, it was made as a political move aimed to abandon rather than withdraw from the entire area of Gaza. It is this political concept that constitutes a dangerous precedent and triggers anxiety.

On the other hand, there yet remains one other opportunity to salvage Jewish land and neutralize its capitulation. This can now be done by a negotiated arrangement by means of which the Palestinians will achieve dignified autonomy, living and working in freedom and tranquility, whereas Israel will retain its Holy Land, as well as its security and independence.

Thus, in spite of errors of judgment on both sides, it is essential for America and Israel to continue their relentless and coordinated war against terror. Together, Bush and Sharon are capable of reducing Moslem radicalism to a minimum. As a result, we may yet see an attempt by the eventually elected Palestinian leadership to build bridges of constructive achievements aimed at improving living conditions for the Palestinian population of Gaza, Judea, and Samaria, as well as tranquility within the borders of the State of Israel.

Though unlikely, it is nevertheless possible that the functioning president of the PLO, Mahmoud Abbas, may yet become a man of goodwill and an apostle of peace. Even if true, this is not enough. The Palestinian dilemma must not be compared to the Iraqi situation. In Iraq, Saddam Hussein's brutality and his anti-Americanism was opposed, resented and secretly confronted by a vast majority of Iraqis. The fact that millions risked their lives to install a new, democratic, pro-American government, attests to this conclusion. But even in Iraq, there remains a powerful opposition that continues to side with Muslim fundamentalism and violent anti-Americanism.

In case of the Palestinians, in addition to Arafat's regime of corruption, terrorism and dictatorship, they, in their masses, have been subjected to education contaminated with hatred of Israel and America for fifty and thirty years respectively. They were taught from childhood the glory of martyrdom and the triumph of suicidal attacks on the infidel. This education has penetrated deeply into the vast majority of Palestinian youths. It will take at least a full generation to eliminate its effect. And it can only be done with a thorough de-radicalization and abolishment of hate propaganda in Arab schools and universities, as well as in books, newspapers, radio and TV. It can not possibly be dictated from above or eliminated by negotiations and optimistic slogans alone.

Until the bacteria of hate are totally exorcised from the new generation, no long term commitments should even be attempted. In the interim period, the goal of the negotiators should be limited to include: 1) tranquility; 2) secured and improved living conditions of the Palestinians; 3) creation of joint ventures between the Palestinians and Israelis.

No doubt there will be serious forces working against any attempt to postpone the ultimate decision on Palestinian independence and statehood. This will make Israel's and America's task that much more difficult. However, no American president had ever understood the true dilemma of the Middle East or the dangerous problems threatening Israel's survival better than President George W. Bush. Likewise, there was no time when the American President and the Israeli Prime Minister understood each other better or cooperated closer.

Therefore, this is the time when it is realistic to anticipate the dawning of a period of constructive stability in the relationship between the Palestinians and the Israelis. It is also time to revive Menachem Begin's concept—accepted by both Egypt and America at Camp David in September 1978—of establishing a "limited autonomy" for the Palestinians living in Gaza, Judea and Samaria today.

Parallel to this, it is becoming increasingly important for the Jewish World to unite under the banner of Herzlian Zionism and, if necessary, to ostracize from within its ranks, the element vociferous in its opposition to Zion's growth, security and welfare. It is imperative for the Jewish populations of Israel and America to give their unreserved support to the present governments of these two allied nations. Such a unity is both foreseeable and possible in the immediate future. To achieve it there must be a clearly declared, generally acceptable goal.

This goal must be neither tarnished by accommodation to popular demand nor obscured by competing interests. Such a goal should be announced to the world immediately and should be based on this premise: A well secured existence and growth of the State of Israel, within defensible borders, living in peace and friendship with its neighbors.

However, the program of action must, of practical necessity, rely on evolutionary rather than revolutionary process.

It must be clearly understood that a new Arab state, bordering with Israel, intent on its destruction, cannot be tolerated. Therefore, it must be resisted at all cost.

On the other hand, a benign, peace aspiring state, interested in living side by side with its neighbor, is a virtual impossibility at this time.

Murderers, fanatics, hate-permeated citizens and suicide bombers constitute the majority of the Palestinian Arab population. Neither they nor their immediate leaders can be partners for peace.

The new Palestinian leadership can succeed only with the prodding of Arab "moderates" (if they can be found) and the careful guidance of the American Government. In anticipation of such a non-belligerent Arab leadership, Israel is gradually returning to the pre-intifada status quo. Eventually, it will have to offer Palestinian Arabs more and more autonomy for more and more cooperation.

When the new leadership takes root, its first priority must be to establish a solid financial and economic base. Its second task must include a radical change of Palestinian educational programs by eliminating all negative references to Israel and the Jews, as well as all Nazi-type propaganda in its press. Likewise, Arab maps will have to include the State of Israel.

Economic, social, cultural and scientific cooperation should gradually replace security committees, which eventually will be placed in the hands of police, coordinating activity from both sides.

A normal period for this gradual evolution would take a generation, or some twenty years. An especially successful program possibly could be achieved in 10 to15 years.

This important intermediary period should be used by the United States and any nation ready to cooperate to fight and win its war against terrorism. Simultaneously, every effort should be made by the United States to help modernize and democratize the Arab world, from Iraq to Iran to Syria and Saudi Arabia.

Only after a successful conclusion of such an evolution could Israel and the Palestinian Arabs sit down to discuss outstanding issues and final borders. By then Arab Palestinians will have learned the full advantages of living in peace and cooperation with Israel and Israel, in turn, will gradually lose its mistrust and fear of negotiating with a "partner" bent on its destruction.

Of course, given the prevalent climate and the destructive influence of the United Nations and the European Union, this process may not have a smooth sailing. Other programs will, no doubt, be initiated. However, they will all fail.

The evolutionary process suggested above will become the only acceptable alternative to more frustration, tragedy and tears. The earlier it is set in motion; the sooner there will be peace and tranquility in the Middle East.

Notes

1. *Election and the Jewish Vote* Article by Jay Lefkowitz, in *Commentary* of February 2005. New York, USA

Chapter 15
Beware of Tomorrow

Remember the *Marranos*? Well to some they remained the heroes that converted to Christianity while secretly retaining their Jewishness. To others, however, they were nothing short of pitiful cowards who, eventually—in their vast majority—submerged into the wave of assimilation and were totally lost to Judaism.

This is indeed an important historic precedent we must never forget. The moment you turn away from your faith and your people—even though this may be done under duress—you place yourself onto a bridge leading to assimilation.

The naked treason of assimilation is often dressed up in various patches of generic garments such as fear, self-preservation, diversification and universalism.

In modern times it began to manifest itself in the German-born Reform movement in Judaism. It soon spread and became popular in the United States of America where, judging by statistics, it became a bridge to assimilation, rather than one bringing the assimilated back into the fold, as originally intended.

During the Holocaust, the extremely poor effort at rescue by the "official" lame leadership of Jewish Communities in the Diaspora was in a way explicable only with the same pathetic excuse of self-preservation.

And this trend follows all the way into the brilliant and difficult days of Israel's independence. Even today, one can trace the underlying cause of Jewish abandonment of its heritage, traditions, history and patriotism, to a covert yearning to become more acceptable and appealing to the world at large. This trend is evident today among many American Jews, who, consciously or not, tend to support Reform over Orthodoxy, the modern Liberalism over conservatism and Israel's New Leftism over the orthodox-nationalism.

There is little wonder then that during the Intifada, Jews of America, in the thousands, found cause for Arab insurrection and blamed the State of Israel for its aggressive self-defense.

But perhaps the most poignant example of the attitude of the Jewish majority in America today is in the declining number of visits to Israel made during the difficult years of the Intifada. It has been estimated that the highest percentage of visitors came from the Jewish Orthodox and Christian evangelist sectors in America. The lowest came from the Reform.

Although there are no scientific statistics available, there is little doubt of an existing connection between the Left, the present day Democrats, the Internationalists and the Jewish Reformists. They all seem to be genetically related and hermetically linked.

It is in this painful correlation among forces which continue to place secular, Liberal values ahead of Jewish interests, that we discover the true cause of Zion's tears today.

From the days of Arlozoroff to the killings on the Altalena, heavy, bitter tears were shed by Zion in remorse for the self inflicted wounds caused by jealousies, divisiveness, duality of goals and surrender to the ideology of internationalism. It is no different in our time.

However, due to their numerous and oft repeated errors, the ultra Left-Liberal Zionists in both Israel and America are diminishing in numbers. Many, once on the slope, continued to roll down into complete assimilation. This element, though lost to both Zionism and Judaism, is not a real loss to the moral values of either.

There is a growing tendency among Jews in Israel and—though to a lesser extent—Jews in America, to close ranks, embrace their heritage, honor their traditions and assert their historical rights.

This change of heart has been made evident by Sharon's victory at the polls and the growing number of Jews who have voted for President George W. Bush.

Of course there will always be weakness, naiveté, cowardice and moronity that will cause tears to Zion. However, these elements, combining evil and agnosticism, are present in every community, among all people. The results of their actions depend on whether they are allowed to dominate or become subdued into irrelevance.

In the meantime, history has turned a full circle. Again, mortal danger faces the State of Israel and the very future of world Jewry. This time, as in the early 1930s, few of us dare speak of the new Holocaust that is being contrived by the Moslem world of fundamentalists. And, unless we act as one, united People, we may well be consumed for eternity.

This mortal danger is the nuclear weapon presently being prepared by Iran, Syria and North Korea, and which is eagerly awaited by the hordes of terrorists anxious to deliver their final blow.

Of course, with America on Israel's side, the balance of forces would remain to Israel's advantage. But even with America's active support, it will be questionable whether Israel's total elimination could be prevented once the weapon becomes operational in Syria's, Iran's or the terrorists' hands.

The window for preventing this catastrophe will remain open as long as George W. Bush remains President of the United States of America. After that, who knows whether he will be replaced by a Reagan-like or a Carter-like Chief of State? In situations of such historic significance, no nation can gamble on a positive outcome. Thus, it becomes essential to destroy any eventual capability among the Arab States to utilize the weapon of mass destruction against the Jewish State.

Of course this drastic route need not be followed in the blessed possibility of a sudden, all consuming revolt within the Arab States, such as is presently brewing in Lebanon. Otherwise, preventive aggression becomes the only solution for Israel's self preservation. In this regard, Norman Podhoretz* writes: "If an uprising is not in the cards, we will be left with only one alternative to pre-emptive military action—standing by (while kidding ourselves with empty motions of diplomacy) and waiting as the world's leading sponsor of terrorism acquires nuclear weapons that it could pass on to its terrorist protégés for use against the 'great Satan'."

There are always the stubborn (and vision impaired) battalions of "peace at all cost" movement, who will again come forward arguing on the basis of the old doctrine of Mutual Assured Destruction, as referred to in the days of the Cold War. However, they ignore the vast gap in the cultural and situational differences between the Soviet Union and Arab extremists. Many renowned appeasers claim that the Iranians would not equip their favored terrorists with nuclear weapons because they would be deterred from doing so by fear that in the event such weapons were actually used, they themselves would become vulnerable to a retaliatory nuclear strike by America. Podhoretz refutes this concept thus: "The obvious problem with this soothing argument is that the Iranian regime would hotly deny any connection to a terrorist attack on us. Nor would our intelligence agencies, burned once over Saddam, likely be so quick to fix the responsibility on them. Under that all-too-plausible scenario, it would be, yes. "MAD" to place our faith in the Mutual Assured Destruction theory." [1]

As far as Israel is concerned, there is no reason to even consider the "MAD" theory. It will take only one, concerted and well planned nuclear attack, to destroy the Jewish State and all its inhabitants. There is no question of retaliation in this event. Therefore, Israel must now speak with one voice and act decisively.

In his article "What Israel Must Do to Survive", Mark Helprin** writes: "If Israel is to survive, it must prepare more assiduously than it has yet done for four types of warfare: political war on the world stage, civil war, conventional war, and a war of weapons of mass destruction. As much as it should try to avoid fighting without benefit of patronage or allies, it must be ready, in extremis, to do so. And despite its long exhaustion it has to prepare its defenses with gravity of a people who once more in modern memory are facing the prospect of destruction." [2]

Admittedly, we are dealing here with two very different scenarios. Their linkage, however, is related to the future of Israel as an independent Jewish State.

One element deals with the global danger of nuclear proliferation in which Israel becomes the prime victim. The other is diplomatic strategy in the event of Israel's successful survival from the nuclear menace. In both, the only reliable partner for Israel is the United States of America, as long as it is being led by positive, conservative elements, such as are leading it today.

On one hand, there is the nuclear threat which must be dealt with immediately, with no consideration of the current diplomatic maneuvering with the new Palestinian leadership.

To deal with this real threat, Israel will be bound to rely on America's success in neutralizing pan-Arab radicalism through a determined and aggressive policy of democratization. Failure to achieve real democratization in Syria and Iran within the immediate future will destroy all existing potential for any peaceful solutions to the existing crisis. In fact it will make it imperative for both Israel and the United States of America to destroy all capability of any Muslim state in the Middle East to acquire or manufacture weapons of mass destruction, be they nuclear or biological.

In the event America's New Left will be able to persuade Bush's Administration to venture onto the path of appeasement and rely on the impotency of the United Nations, Israel, in view of its most vulnerable situation, will be forced to act on its own.

On the other hand, the Palestinian question must be placed on hold within the framework of non-violent co-existence, wherein the Palestinians would enjoy limited autonomy as detailed in previous chapters.

The main danger to this double-edged resolution of the Middle Eastern dilemma is in the possible resurrection of the presently wounded New Left in both Israel and America.

Whatever remains of American Jewry after the long period of assimilation and political affliction with liberalism, must be reunited under the banner of Herzlian Zionism so as to stand solidly behind Israel and its own Government, under President Bush, in order to actively and resolutely defy all attempts of Moslem radicalism to destroy the State of Israel. Indeed, this Muslim radicalism must be prevented from continuing its march aimed at obliterating all remnants of Judeo-Christian values which presently guard the moral and physical safety of the United States of America.

It is time for Jews around the world to turn away from their demi-gods of communism, socialism and new liberalism and to embrace the true spirit of Herzel's Zionism which was created on the solid foundation of Judaism and which remains the only reliable guardian of the Jewish future and the future of Zion.

Only in victory there will be no more bloodshed, no more sorrow and no more tears. . . .

Notes

* Norman Podhoretz is editor-at-large of *Commentary*, a senior fellow at the Hudson Institute, and author of eight books.

** Mark Helprin whose novels include: *Soldier of the Great War*, *Winter's Tale*,

Memoir from Antproof Case and *Refiner's Fire*, is a contributing editor of the *Wall Street Journal*.

1. *The War Against World War IV* Article by Norman Podhoretz in *Commentary*. New York. February 2005.
2. *What Israel Must Do to Survive* by Mark Heprin in *Mideast Peace Process* as edited by Neal Kozoday. Published by Encounter Books. S.F., California.

Index

A.K., 41
Abbas, Mahmoud, 119
Acco jail, 59
Achimeir, Abba, 11
Algemain Zionists, 5
Allon, Yigal, 91
Aloni, Ehudith, 109
American Jewish Committee, 32
Amir, Yigal, 104-105
"Altalena", 8, 63-69, 95, 124
Anilievich, Mordechai, 36
Appelbaum, Mordechai, 36-37, 41
Arab League, 92
Arafat, Yassir, 92-95, 103-104, 112-114, 117, 119
Arens, Moshe, 99-102
Arlozoroff case, 11-17, 95, 104
Arlozoroff, Chaim, 7-8, 11, 124
Asch, Shalom, 20
Assad, Hafez, 92
Autonomy, 91, 102, 119

Balfour Declaration, 14, 16, 20
Baker, James, 101-102
Barak, Ehud, 106, 109, 111-114
Bartal, Israel, 110
Begin, Menachem, 8, 46-47, 50, 54, 56, 59, 63, 66-68, 72-74, 76-77, 81-82, 84, 86, 88-90, 93, 95-96, 105, 116
Beilin, Yossi, 3, 87, 96, 103, 105, 106, 109, 11, 116
Ben Ami, Uda, 27, 30
Ben Eliezer, 27, 47, 48, 64
Ben Gurion, David, 7, 8, 14-15, 21, 25, 45, 48-49, 53, 56, 58, 65, 68, 71-73, 81, 91, 109, 111
Ben Hecht, 28, 29, 30
"Betar", 6, 21, 24, 32, 46, 71, 11, 105
betarim, 11, 12, 13, 16, 27, 36, 42, 46
Bergson's Group, 28-32, 62
Bergson, Peter, 33
Bidault, George, 63
Brandeis, Louis, 27
Bund, 4, 37, 38

Bush, George H.W., 101
Bush, George W., 114, 116, 117, 119, 124, 126
"Bystry", 36, 39, 41

Camp David, 90, 92, 102
Carter, Jimmy, 89, 92
Ceausescu, Nicolae, 90
Chief Rabbinate, 50
Churchill, Winston, 48, 55
Clinton, William, 112, 113
Committee to Save Jewish People of Europe, 28, 31
Cronkite, Walter, 90
Czerniakow, 37

Darwish, Mahmoud, 111
"Davar", 21
Dayan, Moshe, 75-77, 86
Dinur, Benzion, 109
Dir Yassin village, 56-57

Eban, Abba, 76, 94
Eisenhower, Dwight, 73
Einstein, Albert, 20
Eshkol, Levy, 69, 74-77, 81, 91, 94
European Union, 92
evacuation, 19-22

Fatah, 92, 104
Fein, Monroe, 63, 66-68
Fishman, Rabbi J.L., 68

"Gahal", 81, 82, 84
Galili, Israel, 59, 64, 65
Gemayel, Basir, 95
General Zionists, 5, 21, 22, 68, 84
Gillette, Guy, 31
Goldman, Nachum, 31, 72
"Gush Emunim", 105, 116

Hagana, 6, 48-49, 53, 55-59, 62, 63, 65, 68
"Hamas", 92
"havlaga", 45
"Hazbolla", 92
Hertzel, Theodor, 1-4, 75
Herut, 59, 71-74, 76, 81, 84, 116

Heyd, Michael, 110
Histadrut, 71, 115
Holocaust, 27-32, 35, 111, 123, 124
Hussein, Saddam, 119
Hurwitz, Harry, 86, 88

inifada, 113, 114, 123
Irgun Zvai Leumi, 27, 41, 45, 47, 48, 56, 59, 62, 65, 66, 73
Islamic Jihad, 92
Iwansky, Capt., 36

Jabotinsky, Eri, 27
Jabotinsky, Zeev, 5-7, 14, 15, 22, 24, 35, 36, 62, 86, 87, 90, 94, 105
Jaffa, liberation of, 57-58
Jewish Agency, 16, 21, 50, 57
Jewish Army Committee, 28, 30
Jewish Legion, 5, 13
Judenrat, 36, 37, 43

"Kach", 115
Kahan Commission, 95
Kastina airfield, 54
Katz, Shmuel, 64
Kfar, Vitkin, 65, 66, 68
King David Hotel, 54-55
Kissinger, Henry, 83, 85
Kook, Hillel, 27
"Kristal Nacht", 16, 19

Labor Party, 1, 38, 83, 86, 87, 90, 92, 96, 100, 102, 111, 115, 116
Labor Zionists, 6, 7, 11, 50, 65
Landau, Chaim, 64
Lavon affair, 74
Lavon, Pinhas, 74
Lazar, Chaim, 36, 37, 42
Lazarev, Dr., 64
Lerner, Max, 29, 33
Liberal Party, 84, 116
liberals, 82, 84, 105, 124
liberalism, 82, 87, 96, 109, 113, 115, 123, 126
Likud, 85, 86, 89, 90, 96, 99, 100, 102, 104-106, 111, 116, 117

"Maitek", 36, 41
Mapai, 11-12, 14, 21, 58, 62, 71-72, 74, 75, 81-82, 84, 105
Meir, Golda, 14, 74, 75, 76, 81, 82, 85, 86, 91

"Meraz", 87, 96, 102, 105, 112, 115, 116
Meridor, Dan, 101, 106
Meridor, Salai, 100
Meridor, Yaacov, 45, 46, 48, 64, 66
"Mizrachi", 5, 22, 68
Merlin, Shmuel, 67
Morgenthau, Henry, 31
Mubarak, Hosni, 101, 102
"Muranovsky 7", 36, 37, 42

N.S.Z., (National Armed Forces), 44
National Religious Party, 87, 105, 111, 116
nationalists, 5
Nasser, Gamel, 74, 76, 83
new liberalism, 109-110, 115, 116
New Zionist Organization, 16, 21, 23
Netanyahu, Benjamin, 104, 106
Nixon, Richard, 83, 85

Orthodox, 5, 97, 112, 123
orghodoxy, 105, 116, 123
Osiraq plant, 93
Oslo agreement, 103, 105, 111, 118

Palgin, Giddy, 57, 58
Palmach, 49, 66
Patterson, Henry, 5, 13
"Peace Now", 4, 84, 87, 91, 95, 96, 109, 113
"peaceniks", 92
"Peace for Galilee", 94-95
peace plan, 101
PLO, 92, 94-95, 101, 103-104, 106, 113, 119
Peres, Shimon, 1, 75, 86, 91, 93-94, 96, 99-105, 106, 109, 116
Phalangists, 95
"Poalei Zion", 4, 38

Raanan, Mordechai, 49
Rabin, Itzhak, 86, 87, 94, 99-106, 109, 118
Rafi, 75, 83, 84, 86
Ravid, Eliahu, 49
Raziel, David, 45
Reform Movement, 22, 123, 124
Reagan, Ronald, 93
Revisionists, 5, 7, 11, 12, 14, 20, 21, 36, 42, 105
Rogers, Will Jr., 28, 33, 81, 83

Rosenblatt, Zvi, 11, 12, 13
Rosenman, Samuel, 32

Sabra, 95, 96
Sadat, Anwar, 83, 89, 90
Sapir, Pinhas, 83
Sapir, Yosef, 77
Sarid, Yossi, 3, 87, 96, 102, 106, 109, 110, 111, 116
Schechtman, Joseph, 13, 25, 61
"Season", 48-50, 95
settlers, 4
Shamir, Itzhak, 96, 99, 101, 102, 103
Sharett, Moshe, 74
Shapiro, Moshe, 68
"Shas", 102, 112
Sharansky, Natan, 111, 112
Sharon, Ariel, 84-85, 93, 95, 114, 116, 117, 118, 124
Shatila, 95, 96
Shilansky, Dov, 73
Shultz, George, 99, 100
Shkolnik, Levi, 64
Silver, Abba, 27
Sne, Moshe, 54
socialists, 5
Stavsky, Abraham, 11, 12, 13, 62, 63, 66, 67
Stern Group, 47, 48, 51, 53, 56
Straits of Tiran, 74, 75
Stroop, Jurgen, 39, 40

Tavin, Eli, 49
Tnuat, Hameri, (The United Resistance Movement), 53, 54
Trumpeldor, Yosef, 5, 6

United Nations, 62, 74, 92, 93, 113, 117, 120, 126

Vaze, Pinhas, 64, 65

Walewski, Dr. R., 40
War Refugee Board, 31
Warsaw Ghetto Uprising, 36-43, 111
Weizmann, Chaim, 23, 24, 45, 48, 49, 84
Weizman, Ezer, 84
Wise, Stephen, 21, 24, 27, 30, 31
World Zionist Organization, 25

Yom Kippur War, 85-86, 87, 94

Zimmerman, Moshe, 110
Zionist Congress, 7, 13, 75, 106
Zionist Organization, 7, 21, 22
ZOB (Jewish Fighting Organization), 36, 39, 41
Zucherman, Yitzhak, 39
ZZW (Jewish Military Organization), 36, 39, 41, 42

About the Author

Ya'acov (Yana) Liberman was born in 1923 in Harbin, China. It was there that he adopted Jabotinsky's Zionist-Revisionist philosophy as his ideology and way of life.

In his early days, Yana became the leader of the Betar Youth Movement, which led him to occupy prominent positions within the nationalistic Revisionist Party. Eventually, Ya'acov became Menachem Begin's right hand man as chairman of Israel's Herut Party organizational department and leader of Israel's Betar.

In 1948, Liberman was placed in charge of the first shipload of immigrants to Israel, leading some eight hundred passengers on a historic journey from Shanghai to Haifa, lasting 52 days!

By 1965, he was able to resume his post-graduate studies in Tokyo while working as a manager of an international trading company there. In 1968, Ya'acov graduated with honors from Sophia University, obtaining a major's degree in political science.

During these years, Liberman continuously wrote political articles on the Middle East problems for dailies and periodicals in Israel, U.S., Australia and South Africa. He also authored a three-act play *"Mechoratai" (My Country)* and two books: *From One Jew to Another* and *My China*, dedicated to Jewish life in China during the first half of the twentieth century.

The Liberman family is now living in San Diego, California.

www.ingramcontent.com/pod-product-compliance
Lightning Source LLC
Chambersburg PA
CBHW021833300426
44114CB00009BA/425